Langua Links

Grammar and vocabulary for self-study

ADRIAN DOFF AND CHRISTOPHER JONES

BEGINNER > ELEMENTARY

CAMBRIDGE
UNIVERSITY PRESS

CAMBRIDGE UNIVERSITY PRESS
Cambridge, New York, Melbourne, Madrid, Cape Town, Singapore, São Paulo

Cambridge University Press
The Edinburgh Building, Cambridge CB2 2RU, UK

www.cambridge.org
Information on this title: www.cambridge.org/9780521523974

First published 2005

Printed in Great Britain by BemroseBooth, Derby

A catalogue record for this book is available from the British Library

ISBN-13 978-0-521-52397-4 paperback
ISBN-10 0-521-52397-4

ISBN-13 978-0-521-52400-1 paperback and audio CD pack
ISBN-10 0-521-52400-8

Contents

Numbers (1)

1–100; two hundred, five thousand, a million …

A Vocabulary one, two, three …

1	one	6	six	11	eleven	16	sixteen
2	two	7	seven	12	twelve	17	seventeen
3	three	8	eight	13	thirteen	18	eighteen
4	four	9	nine	14	fourteen	19	nineteen
5	five	10	ten	15	fifteen	20	twenty

1 Write the numbers 1–10 in the crossword.

2 Write the numbers. The person wants …

a ___thirteen___ sandwiches.

b _____ burgers.

c _____ hot drinks.

d _____ cold drinks.

e _____ cakes.

f _____ pizzas.

Links

cup of …,
bottle of … ➲14B
burger, pizza … ➲43A
coffee, tea … ➲42A

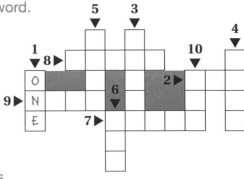

I'd like six Mega burgers, five cheeseburgers, five Napoli pizzas, nine Mega pizzas, ~~four chicken sandwiches, nine cheese sandwiches,~~ ten chocolate cakes, nine lemon cakes, seven cups of coffee, eight bottles of lemonade, seven bottles of water and five cups of tea.

B Vocabulary twenty, thirty, forty …

20	twenty	60	sixty	21	twenty-one	26	twenty-six
30	thirty	70	seventy	22	twenty-two	27	twenty-seven
40	forty	80	eighty	23	twenty-three	28	twenty-eight
50	fifty	90	ninety	24	twenty-four	29	twenty-nine
		100	a hundred	25	twenty-five		

3 Write the next *two* numbers.

   a fifty-five, sixty, sixty-five, _seventy_ , _seventy-five_

   b forty-five, forty-seven, forty-nine, _____ , _____

   c ninety-two, ninety-one, ninety, _____ , _____

   d fifty-six, fifty-seven, fifty-eight, _____ , _____

   e forty-four, forty-two, forty, _____ , _____

4 Complete the sentences. Write the numbers as words.

Links

I'm, it's, is   ➦58

euros   ➦33A

   a I'm _twenty-one_ today.

   b It's nine _____ .

   c John's house is number _____ .

   d The bus is number _____ .

   e It's _____ kilometres to Berlin.

   f It's _____ euros _____ .

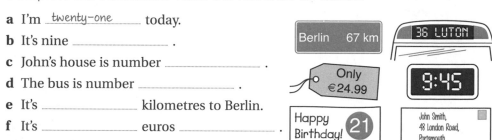

C Vocabulary   Large numbers

1800–1950	1,000 km	$10,000,000
= a hundred and fifty **years**	= a thousand **kilometres**	= ten million **dollars**

100	a hundred	200	two hundred	1,000	a thousand
110	a hundred and ten	250	two hundred and fifty	10,000	ten thousand
150	a hundred and fifty	500	five hundred	1,000,000	a million

! a hundred and ten, NOT ~~one hundred ten~~
two hundred and fifty, NOT ~~two hundred fifty~~
two hundred, NOT ~~two hundreds~~; ten thousand, NOT ~~ten thousands~~

5 Write the numbers as words.

Link

dollars, euros   ➦33A

   a _five hundred_ euros

   b _____ metres

   c _____ people

   d _____ litres

   e _____ years

   f _____ dollars

   g _____ grams

London–Bangkok: *only* €500

50,000 PEOPLE AT FREE CONCERT

PARKING ☞ 2,000 metres

about 3,000 years

WIN $1,000,000

650 grams of flour

5,000,000 litres of water

Write in your language

Is he twelve or thirteen?	
It's sixty-six kilometres to London.	
It's twenty thousand dollars.	

Numbers (2)

first, second, third ...; on the (fifth) floor; 14th July / the 14th of July

A Vocabulary **first, second, third ...**

Link
➲1 Numbers (1)

Curtis is first,   ... Oatway is second, ... and Ivanov is third, ...

1st	first	6th	sixth	11th	eleventh	16th	sixteenth
2nd	second	7th	seventh	12th	twelfth	17th	seventeenth
3rd	third	8th	eighth	13th	thirteenth	18th	eighteenth
4th	fourth	9th	ninth	14th	fourteenth	19th	nineteenth
5th	fifth	10th	tenth	15th	fifteenth	20th	twentieth

Word	Number	Word	Number
first	➡ 1st	fourth	➡ 4th
second	➡ 2nd	tenth	➡ 10th
third	➡ 3rd	twentieth	➡ 20th

1 Complete the sentences. Write the numbers as words.

a Is Sunday the _first_ [1st] day of the week
or the _____ [7th] day of the week?

b It's her _____ [18th] birthday tomorrow.

c This is my _____ [15th] cup of coffee today.

d The _____ [1st] prize is a car, the
_____ [2nd] prize is a holiday, and
the _____ [3rd] prize is €100.

B Phrases **on the fourth floor**

Links
on   ➲20A
floor   ➲35C

Our flat is on the fourth floor.

on the	first fourth tenth ...	floor

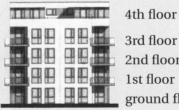

4th floor
3rd floor
2nd floor
1st floor
ground floor

2 Which floor? Complete the sentences.

a The café is on the fifth floor.

b Men's clothes are _____

c There's a restaurant

_____

d John Smith lives

_____

e Room 135 is _____

f The Yoga Centre is _____

g There's a swimming pool _____

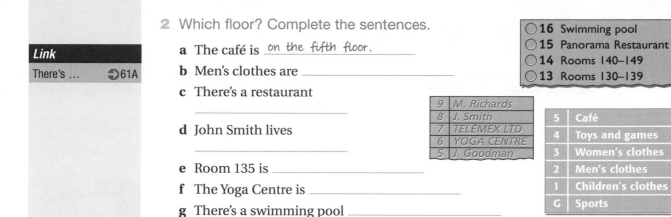

○ **16** Swimming pool
○ **15** Panorama Restaurant
○ **14** Rooms 140–149
○ **13** Rooms 130–139

9	M. Richards
8	J. Smith
7	TELEMEX LTD
6	YOGA CENTRE
5	J. Goodman

5	Café
4	Toys and games
3	Women's clothes
2	Men's clothes
1	Children's clothes
G	Sports

Link

There's … ➲61A

C Phrases

Dates

Link

December, April ➲6A

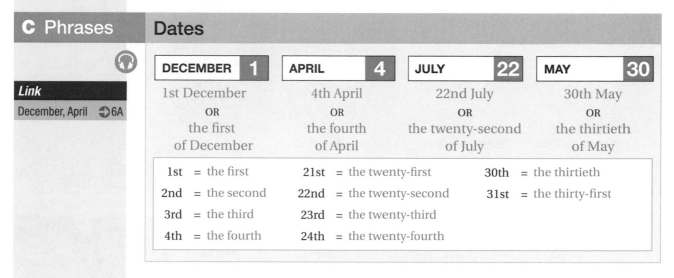

DECEMBER **1**	APRIL **4**	JULY **22**	MAY **30**
1st December	4th April	22nd July	30th May
OR	OR	OR	OR
the first of December	the fourth of April	the twenty-second of July	the thirtieth of May

1st = the first
2nd = the second
3rd = the third
4th = the fourth

21st = the twenty-first
22nd = the twenty-second
23rd = the twenty-third
24th = the twenty-fourth

30th = the thirtieth
31st = the thirty-first

3 Look at the woman's diary. Answer the questions.

a When is she going to the Music Festival?
  On the twenty-second of May.

b When is she going on holiday?
  On _____

c When are her children going to France?
  _____

d When is her mother's birthday?
  _____

e When is she going to the doctor?
  _____

f When is she seeing Nick?
  _____

Links

on ➲5A
When …? ➲79C
is …-ing ➲69, 71

May–June		June	
21		4	Lunch with Mary
22		5	
23	MUSIC	6	Nick
24	FESTIVAL	7	
25		8	
26		9	
27	Dr Bell	10	Car
28		11	
29		12	Mum's birthday
30		13	
31	HOLIDAY	14	Children to France
1		15	
2		16	London
3		17	London

Write in your language

When is your twenty-fifth birthday?	
They live on the fourteenth floor.	
I'm coming on the thirty-first of July.	

3 Time (1)

It's (one) o'clock; half past, quarter to/past; five past, ten past …; What's the time?

A Phrases It's eight o'clock

Link
➡1   **Numbers (1)**

It's eight o'clock in New York.　It's two o'clock in Rome.　It's six o'clock in Karachi.　It's ten o'clock in Tokyo.

1 What time is it in these places?

a <u>It's five o'clock</u> in Los Angeles.

b _____ in London.

c _____ in Beirut.

d _____ in Rio de Janeiro.

e _____ in Singapore.

f _____ in Sydney.

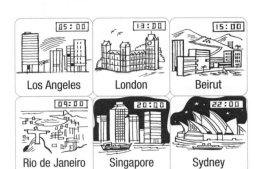

Los Angeles 05:00　London 13:00　Beirut 15:00

Rio de Janeiro 09:00　Singapore 20:00　Sydney 22:00

B Phrases It's half past eight

Link
it's   ➡58C

It's half past eight.　It's quarter past one.　It's quarter to six.

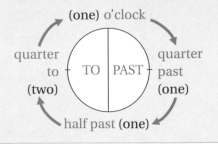

(one) o'clock

quarter to (two)　TO | PAST　quarter past (one)

half past (one)

2 Put the words in the correct order. Match them with the clocks.

a four it's past quarter　<u>It's quarter past four.</u>　Clock [3]

b it's past seven half　_____　Clock [ ]

c five to quarter it's　_____　Clock [ ]

d past quarter it's ten　_____　Clock [ ]

e twelve past half it's　_____　Clock [ ]

1 10:15　**2** 　**3** 　**4** 　**5**

C Phrases *It's five past three*

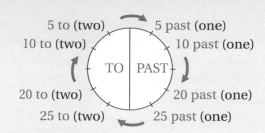

5 to (two)   5 past (one)
10 to (two)   10 past (one)

TO | PAST

20 to (two)   20 past (one)
25 to (two)   25 past (one)

It's five past three.   It's twenty past six.   It's ten to four.

3 Write the missing times.

a four o'clock, five past four, _ten past four_, quarter past four

b quarter to six, ten to six, _____ , six o'clock

c quarter past ten, twenty past ten, _____ , half past ten

d quarter to nine, _____ , five to nine, nine o'clock

e half past two, twenty-five to three, _____ , quarter to three

D Phrases *What time is it?*

Links

What ...?   ➜ 79B
about   ➜ 8B

What time is it?   It's one o'clock.   What's the time?   It's about quarter past six.

4 Complete the questions and answers.

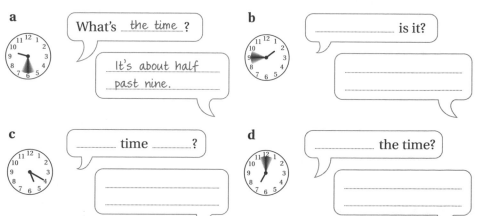

a What's _the time_?

It's about half past nine.

b _____ is it?

_____

c _____ time _____?

_____

d _____ the time?

_____

Write in your language

What time is it?	
It's about half past five.	
It's quarter to two.	

4 Time (2)

two ten, two thirty …; at (six thirty) in the (morning); before (work), after (lunch)

A Vocabulary — *half past two = two thirty*

Links

⤴3   **Time (1)**
⤴1   **Numbers (1)**

2.10	ten past two	OR	two ten
2.15	quarter past two	OR	two fifteen
2.30	half past two	OR	two thirty
2.40	twenty to three	OR	two forty
2.45	quarter to three	OR	two forty-five

1 Match the times with the clocks.

a   **b**   **c**   **d**   **e**

☐ half past nine	☐ four fifteen
☐ twenty past nine	[a] eleven fifty
☐ quarter past four	☐ nine twenty
[a] ten to twelve	☐ five thirty-five
☐ twenty-five to six	☐ nine thirty

B Phrases — *at eight o'clock*

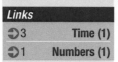

Links

open, close   ⤴34C
verb + -s   ⤴63B

OPEN
8·00 am
– 6·00 pm

CONCERT
Beethoven
Sonatas

8.30–10.30

The shop opens at eight o'clock.
It closes at six o'clock.

The concert starts at eight thirty.
It finishes at ten thirty.

2 Complete the sentences.

Link

get up, go to bed
    ⤴55A

a The swimming pool opens _at ten thirty._
    It closes _____
b The party starts _____
    It finishes _____
c She goes to work _____
    She comes home _____
d He gets up _____
    He goes to bed _____

a SWIMMING POOL OPEN TODAY 10.30 – 5.15
b BIRTHDAY PARTY! 5.00 – 7.30

C Phrases — *at eight o'clock in the morning*

The train leaves Milan at eight o'clock in the morning.

The train leaves Paris at eight o'clock in the morning.

It arrives in Milan at three thirty in the afternoon …

… and it arrives in Rome at nine o'clock in the evening.

Links

morning, afternoon …
➲5C

leaves, arrives ➲31C

Paris....................	08.00
↓	
Milan	15.30
↓	
Rome............	21.00

3 Look at the timetable. Complete the sentences.

a The train arrives in Istanbul
at seven o'clock in the evening.

b It leaves Sinaia

c It arrives in Frankfurt

d It leaves Budapest

e It leaves Paris

f It arrives in Bucharest

TIMETABLE		
Day 1	PARIS	15:40
	FRANKFURT	07:30
Day 2	BUDAPEST	16:50
Day 3	SINAIA	06:30
	BUCHAREST	11:30
	ISTANBUL	19:00

D Phrases — *before work, after dinner*

Avril does a lot of sport. Look at her day.

Links

breakfast, lunch,
dinner ➲44A

go swimming,
play tennis ➲30

go for …,
go …-ing ➲50C

breakfast | W O R K | dinner

7.00 ↑ 9.00 | 1.00 | 5.00 | 7.00 ↑

She goes swimming. | lunch | She goes for a walk.

She goes swimming before work.
She goes for a walk after dinner.

	breakfast
before	lunch
after	dinner
	work

4 Rewrite the words in *italics*. Use words from the table.

a Avril has a cold shower *at 6.30 in the morning.*   before breakfast

b She plays tennis *at 5.30 in the afternoon.*

c She goes running *at 6.30 in the evening.*

d She goes for a walk *at 7.30 in the morning.*

e She plays table tennis *at 1.30 in the afternoon.*

f She does exercises *at 6.45 in the morning.*

Write in your language

The shop opens at 8.30.	
I get up at 6 o'clock in the morning.	
She goes home after lunch.	

5 Days

on (Friday), at the weekend; every (Monday); in the (morning), at night; on (Friday evening)

A Phrases — *on Monday, at the weekend*

Link
at home, at work
➡ 22C

… Yes, I'm at home on Tuesday … No, I'm at work on Friday, and then I'm in London at the weekend …

on	Monday
	Tuesday
	…

at	the weekend

the weekend

Links
They're …-ing ➡ 71A
go to ➡ 50B

1 Some American tourists are going to Europe for a week. Complete the sentences.

a They're going to London ___on Wednesday.___
b They're going to Venice _____
c They're going to Athens _____
d They're going to Rome _____
e They're going back to the USA _____
f They're going to Paris _____

Europe in 7 Days!

Wed	Thurs
London	Paris
Fri	Sat/Sun
Venice	Rome
Mon	Tue
Athens	USA

B Phrases — *every day*

Links
day ➡ 7A
There's … ➡ 61A

MON	8.00–8.00
TUE	8.00–8.00
WED	8.00–8.00
THU	8.00–8.00
FRI	8.00–8.00
SAT	8.00–6.00
SUN	9.00–2.00

Friday Market

Mon	Tue	Wed	Thu	Fri	Sat	Sun
					football	

Mon	Tue	Wed	Thu	Fri	Sat	Sun
					football	

Mon	Tue	Wed	Thu	Fri	Sat	Sun
					football	

This shop is open every day.

There's a market every Friday.

He plays football every weekend.

2 Complete the sentences.

a There's a boat to Paxos ___every Tuesday.___
b We have English _____
c There's a film _____
d The pool is open _____
e There's a concert _____
f They have live music _____

Tuesday 8.00 PAXOS

Tues 8.00–9.00	Maths
Wed 8.00–9.00	English
Thurs 8.00–9.00	Science

8.00 THE SUNDAY FILM: *The Beach* Leonardo DiCaprio

Swimming pool opening hours:
Mon–Fri 3.00–8.00
Sat: 4.00–6.00
Sun: 10.00–3.00

CONCERTS
Fri 8 May: Beethoven, Bach
Fri 15 May: Corelli, Vivaldi
Fri 22nd May: Chopin, Liszt

Café

Sat + Sun Live! Music

C Phrases — *in the morning, at night*

Link
work　⮕29A

These people work for Central Taxis.

Nick works in the morning.

Bob works in the afternoon.

Lynne works in the evening.

John works at night.

in	the morning the afternoon the evening	at night

Central Taxis

6.00	12.00	6.00	12.00	6.00
Nick	Bob	Lynne	John	

3 Six other people work for Central Taxis. Write their names in the table. Complete the sentences below.

Links
doesn't　⮕65A
before, after　⮕4D

- Ali sees Lynne at work.
- Bill sees Nick at work.
- Carlos starts work at 12.00.
- Steve starts work at 6.00.
- Mary doesn't work at night.
- Sue works after Bill, but before Steve.

6.00	12.00	6.00	12.00	6.00
Nick	Bob	Lynne	John
		Ali	

a Ali _works in the evening._

b Carlos _____

c Steve _____

d Mary _____

e Sue _____

f Bill _____

D Phrases — *on Tuesday morning*

I'm playing tennis on Tuesday.

I'm playing tennis in the morning.

→ I'm playing tennis on Tuesday morning.

4 Look at the notes. Complete the sentences.

a He's seeing Olga _on Tuesday afternoon._

b He's going to a party _____

c He's going to a meeting _____

d He's going to a concert _____

e He's seeing the doctor _____

f He's playing tennis _____

MEETING at Transco (Mr Thomas) 9.30 Fri

Olga 2.30 Tues

John's party: Sat 9.00

Concert Wed 8.00

DOCTOR 11.00 MON

TENNIS Sun 4.30

Write in your language

We're going to London on Thursday.	
There's a concert every Friday.	
There's a party on Saturday evening.	

6 Months and seasons

January, February, March …; spring, summer, autumn, winter; in (May), in the (summer)

A Vocabulary Months

1	January	5	May	9	September
2	February	6	June	10	October
3	March	7	July	11	November
4	April	8	August	12	December

1 Write the missing months.

a January, February, _March_

b September, October, _____

c April, May, _____

d July, _____, September

e _____, _____, February

f _____, _____, July

B Phrases *in February*

His birthday is in February.

They're getting married in July.

2 Look at this man's year planner. Complete the sentences.

a He's going to Zurich
  in June.

b He's starting a new job

  _____

c His wife is going to Brazil

  _____

d His son is going to France

  _____

e The family is going on holiday

  _____

f His son is having a party

  _____

g His sister is staying with him

  _____

Links

He's …-ing ➔71

wife, son, sister ➔28A

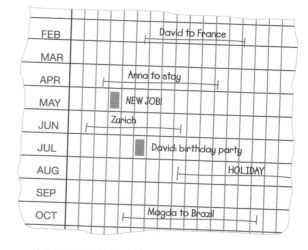

FEB	David to France
MAR	
APR	Anna to stay
MAY	▮ NEW JOB!
JUN	Zurich
JUL	▮ David: birthday party
AUG	HOLIDAY
SEP	
OCT	Magda to Brazil

Seasons

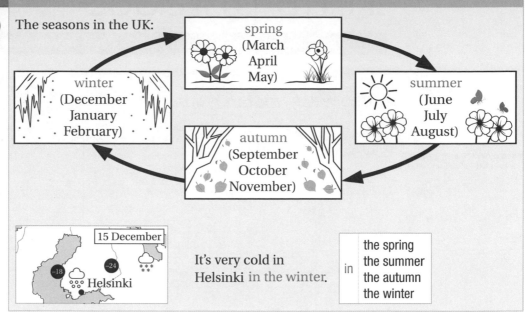

The seasons in the UK:

spring
(March
April
May)

summer
(June
July
August)

winter
(December
January
February)

autumn
(September
October
November)

15 December

−18   −24

Helsinki

It's very cold in
Helsinki in the winter.

in	the spring
	the summer
	the autumn
	the winter

Links

cold, hot, warm ➡38B

very, quite ➡45B

3 Rewrite the sentences. Use words from the table.

a The UK is cold *in January and February*.   The UK is cold in the winter.

b I'm getting married *in October or November*.

c They're going to England *in March or April*.

d Greece is very hot *in July and August*.

e We go skiing *in December or January*.

f It's quite warm here *in April and May*.

4 Write answers 2–11 in the diagram.

Links

month, year ➡7A

before, after ➡4D

first, 2nd, 11th, 12th
➡2A

12

1 The 2nd month ▶ | F | E | B | R | U | A | R | Y |

2 The month after September ▶

3 The season before winter ▶

4 The month before April ▶

5 Hot season ▶

6 The 12th month of the year ▶

7 The first month of the year ▶

8 The season after winter ▶

9 The 11th month ▶

10 Cold season ▶

11 The month before September ▶

Now complete the sentence: **12▼** There are _____ in a year.

Write in your language

My birthday is in August.	
We're going on holiday in the summer.	
They're getting married in the spring.	

7 Time phrases

day, week, month, year; this/next (Friday); today, tomorrow, this morning ...

A Vocabulary · *day, week, month, year*

Links

Monday, Tuesday ...
⮕5A

March ⮕6A

This is a week
in March, 2005.

MARCH	2005	2005	MARCH
14 Monday			17 Thursday
15 Tuesday			18 Friday
16 Wednesday			19 Saturday
			20 Sunday

month

year

day

Links

a week, weeks
⮕10A

There are ... ⮕61A

1 Complete the sentences. Use words from the box.

a There are 365 _days_ in _a year_ .

b There are 52 _____ in _____ .

c There are 28, 29, 30 or 31 _____ in _____ .

d There are 12 _____ in _____ .

e There are 7 _____ in _____ .

a week	days	a month
months	weeks	a year

B Phrases · *this Friday, next summer*

Links

this ⮕13

summer ⮕6C

It's Tuesday 2nd March ...

TODAY   this Friday

	M	Tu	W	Th	F	Sa	Su
this **week** →	1	②	3	4	⑤	6	7
next **week** →	8	9	10	11	⑫	13	14

next Friday

	Monday, Tuesday, ...
this	March, April, ...
next	spring, summer, ...
	week, month, year

2 Match the sentences with the times. Write numbers 1–6.

Link

I'm ...-ing,
We're ...-ing ⮕71A

a [6] I'm going to France next summer.

b [ ] They're coming to stay this October.

c [ ] We're playing tennis next Thursday.

d [ ] I'm going swimming this Friday.

e [ ] He's starting a new job next April.

f [ ] We're staying at home this summer.

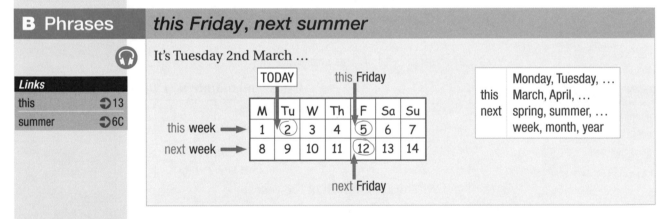

3 Look at the examples. Write about you.

I'm

....

....

....

....

> I'm going to the theatre this Saturday.
>
> I'm going on holiday this October.
>
> I'm buying a car next week.

C Phrases

Links

morning, afternoon …	➲5C
see, hear	➲52A
You can …	➲76A
There's …	➲61A

this morning, tomorrow evening …

There's a children's concert this morning.
You can hear Indian music tomorrow afternoon.
You can see the Bill Ryley band tomorrow evening.
There's a disco tonight.

MUSIC FESTIVAL

TODAY		TOMORROW	
9.00	Children's concert	9.00	*Vienna Strings:* Waltzes by Strauss
11.00	*Jack Munroe:* Scottish Folk Music	10.30	Jazz in the Park
2.00	Carmen Ortega: Spanish Flamenco	2.00	*Alpaca:* Folk music from Peru
4.00	*The Chicago Sound:* 'Singing the Blues'	4.00	*Osman Harishi:* Music from India
7.30	City Orchestra: Mozart Symphony No. 40	8.00	*Bill Ryley Band:* 50s Big Band Music
11.30	DISCO	12.00	STREET PARTY

Today		
this morning (7.00–12.00)	this afternoon (12.00–6.00)	this evening (6.00–11.00)
tonight (11.00–…)		

Tomorrow		
tomorrow morning (7.00–12.00)	tomorrow afternoon (12.00–6.00)	tomorrow evening (6.00–11.00)
tomorrow night (11.00–…)		

4 Complete the sentences.

a You can see Carmen Ortega *this afternoon.*

b You can see Alpaca ....

c You can hear Scottish folk music ....

d There's a Mozart concert ....

e You can hear The Chicago Sound ....

f There's a street party ....

g There's a jazz concert ....

Write in your language

I'm going swimming next Saturday.	
We're getting married next April.	
There's a party tomorrow evening.	

25

8 Age

He's ten (years old); She's nearly/about/over (50); How old ...?

A Phrases

He's ten years old

Link

➜1   Numbers (1)

Links

son, daughter   ➜28A

he's, she's   ➜58C

My **son** is ten years old,
and my **daughter** is eight.

He's ten. OR	**He's** ten years old.
She's eight. OR	**She's** eight years old.

1 Look at the birthday cards. Complete the sentences.

a   **b**   **c**   **d**    **e**   **f**

a She's ___twenty years old.___   **d** She's _____

b She's _____   **e** He's _____

c He's _____   **f** He's _____

B Vocabulary   nearly, about, over

Link

about   ➜33B

Sarah is nearly 30.
(= She's 28 or 29.)

John is about 50.
(= He's 48–52.)

Alice is over 80.
(= She's 80+.)

I'm	nearly	30.
He's	about	50.
She's	over	

2 Rewrite the numbers. Use **nearly**, **about** or **over**.

a John is *37–38* ___nearly 40.___   **d** Her husband is *57–63* _____

b Alec is *28–32* _____   **e** Their son is *18–19* _____

c Maria is *100+* _____   **f** Our teacher is *40+* _____

Link

her, their, our, my ➜19

3 Look at the examples. Write about you and your family and friends.

I'm _____

My _____

My _____

My _____

My _____

> I'm 32 years old.
> My sister is nearly 30.
> My father is over 60.
> My friend Jane is about 40.

C Phrases

He's five days old

Link

day, week, month,
year ➲7A

He's ...   ... five **days**   ... five **weeks**   ... five **months**   ... five
                 old.   old.   old.   **years** old.

4 Complete the sentences. Use words from the box.

three days	100 years
six weeks	500 years ✓
ten months	4,500 years

a It's <u>500 years old.</u>

b She's _____

c It's _____

d They're _____

e It's _____

f It's _____

a   **b**   **c**

d   **e**   **f**

D Phrases

How old ...?

Links

How ...? ➲80B
is/are ➲60B

How old are **you**?   I'm 28.   Do you have a car?   Yes, we do.

How old are
your children?   Six and four.   How old is it?   About five years old.

5 Write questions. Use words from the box.

a <u>How old is your son?</u>

He's 11.

you	your house	your parents
✓ your son	your sister	

b _____

My mother's 62 and my father's 66.

c _____

She's 36.

d _____

I'm nearly 33.

e _____

It's about 50 years old.

Write in your language

He's about 30.	
Our house is over 100 years old.	
How old are you?	

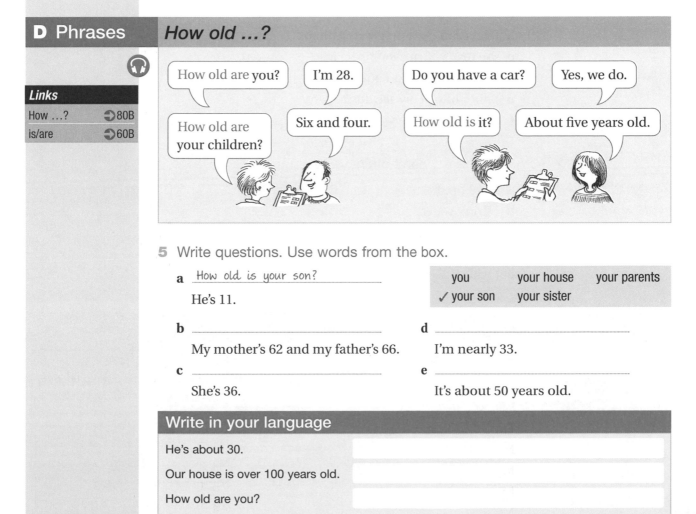

9 Frequency

often, not often; always, sometimes, never; usually, not usually

A Grammar — *often, not often*

Link
➲ 64, 65
Present simple (2), (3)

Link
rain, snow ➲ 38C

In England,
it often rains.

In Egypt, it
doesn't often rain.

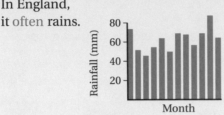

Manchester, England

Alexandria, Egypt

often + verb
It often rains.

not + often + verb
It doesn't often rain.

1 Put the words in the correct order to make sentences.

a often winter the snows in it   It often snows in the winter.

b television don't they watch often

c the reads often evening he in

d Saturday go out on often we

e father often I my see don't

f doesn't jeans she wear often

2 Add **often** or **don't often**. Write about you.

a I feel tired.   I often feel tired. OR I don't often feel tired.

b I drink water.

c I go to the cinema.

d I wear black clothes.

e I watch television.

B Grammar — *always, sometimes, never*

Link
at night ➲ 5C

Dr Lee always works at night.
Dr Hamid sometimes works at night.
Dr Schmidt never works at night.

I	always	
He/She	sometimes	+ verb
…	never	

MERTON HOSPITAL SEPTEMBER: Night duty (10.00 p.m.–6.00 a.m.)				
	Week 1	Week 2	Week 3	Week 4
Dr Lee	✓	✓	✓	✓
Dr Hamid		✓		✓
Dr Schmidt				

ALWAYS ◄————————— SOMETIMES ——————————► NEVER
(= 100%)   (= 0%)

3 Complete the questionnaire. Then write about you.

Links

read, listen to ➔55B

wake up, go to sleep ➔55A

before, after ➔4D

a <u>I sometimes read in bed.</u>

b ....

c ....

d ....

e ....

f ....

g ....

HOW DO YOU SLEEP AT NIGHT? Tick (✓) the boxes.	ALWAYS	SOMETIMES	NEVER
a I read in bed.		✓	
b I listen to music in bed.			
c I sleep with the window open.			
d I sleep with the door open.			
e I wake up in the night.			
f I go to sleep before 12.00.			
g I get up after 8.00.			

C Grammar *usually, not usually*

Links

dress, skirt ... ➔27A

wear, wears ➔63

don't (wear), doesn't (wear) ➔64, 65

What do you wear at work?

I usually wear a dress or a skirt. I don't usually wear trousers, and I never wear jeans.

ALWAYS	100%
USUALLY	
NOT USUALLY	
NEVER	0%

I usually (wear) ...
He/She usually (wears) ...

I don't
He/She doesn't   usually (wear) ...

4 Read the conversation. Complete the sentences. Use **always**, **(not) usually** or **never**.

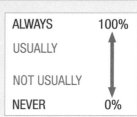

'What do you wear at work?'

'Trousers, usually grey trousers, and a jacket. In the summer, I often wear a shirt and tie, but no jacket.'

'Do you always wear a tie?'

'Well, in very hot weather, I wear a shirt, but no tie.'

'Do you ever wear a jumper?'

'Yes – in *very* cold weather.'

'Do you sometimes wear jeans?'

'Jeans at work? No!'

a The man <u>doesn't usually wear</u> a jumper.

b He .... trousers.

c He .... grey trousers.

d He .... jeans.

e He .... a tie.

f He .... a shirt.

Write in your language

They often go out in the evening.	
He never goes to sleep before 12.00.	
I don't usually wear jeans at work.	

10 Singular and plural

car, cars; -s, -es, -ies, -ves; men, women, children, people

A Grammar — *a table, tables*

Link
→11   *a, an, some*

a table and a chair

Singular (= 1)	
a	table
one	chair

tables and chairs

Plural (= 2, 3, 4, …)	
two	tables
some	chairs
twenty	

Link
plate, bowl, spoon
→44C

1 Choose the right form.

For the children's party, we need a large
(a) *(table)* / ~~tables~~ , and some (b) *chair / chairs* .
We need one large (c) *plate / plates* for the cake,
12 small (d) *plate / plates* , and some small
(e) *bowl / bowls* and (f) *spoon / spoons* for the
ice cream. We need six (g) *bottle / bottles* of
lemonade and some (h) *flower / flowers* for the
table. And we need a (i) *CD player / CD players* …

B Grammar — *cars, boxes, lorries, shelves*

Links
bus, car, taxi   →31A
brush, comb   →40A

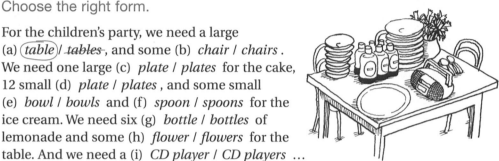

shelves   dictionaries   photos   lorries   buses

brushes   taxis   cars

boxes   glasses   plates   knives

matches   forks

combs

2 Complete the tables.

+ -s	
car	cars
fork	
photo	
comb	
plate	
taxi	

-s, -ch, -x, -sh → + -es	
box	boxes
bus	
glass	
brush	
match	

-y → -ies	
dictionary	dictionaries
lorry	

-f, -fe → -ves	
shelf	shelves
knife	

Links

nurse, secretary ➲29A

fax, letter ➲32A

3 Write the plurals of these words.

a	park	*parks*	**e**	secretary	**i**	watch
b	beach	*beaches*	**f**	church	**j**	fax
c	dress		**g**	wife	**k**	shop
d	nurse		**h**	letter	**l**	baby

C Grammar — People

Link

people ➲25

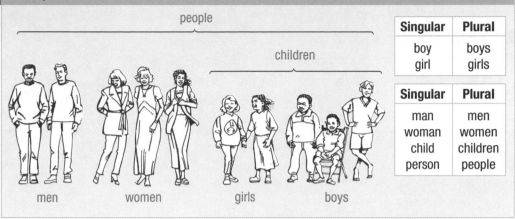

people

children

Singular	Plural
boy	boys
girl	girls

Singular	Plural
man	men
woman	women
child	children
person	people

men   women   girls   boys

4 Complete the sentences.

In the picture, there are …

a three *men*

b four

c five

d six

e eleven

f eighteen

5 Correct the mistakes in these sentences.

a There are five ~~lorrys~~ *lorries* in the car park.

b Those aren't taxies – they're cars.

c I have two English dictionary's.

d They have three childrens: two boys and a girl.

e The books are on the shelfs in the living room.

f There aren't any knifes or forks.

g There are three boxs of knives.

h Who are the peoples in these photoes?

Write in your language

There aren't any buses after 10.00.	
He reads a lot of books.	
I can see four people: two men and two women.	

11 *a, an, some*

a (banana), an (apple); a black dress, black shoes; some (apples)

A Grammar — *a girl, an ice cream*

Link

egg, banana, apple …
➔ 42

In this picture, there's a girl, a hat, an ice cream, an umbrella and a tree.

In this picture, there's a man, an egg, a banana, an apple and an orange.

a + consonant sounds /b, m, t …/
an + vowel sounds /e, i, o …/

a	an
a girl	an ice cream

1 Complete the table.

2 Look at these animals. Write **a** or **an**.

 a *an* elephant

 b .... dog

 c .... antelope

 d .... octopus

 e .... horse

 f .... iguana

B Grammar — *a young man, an old man*

Links

young, old … ➔ 45A

with ➔ 25C

German, American … ➔ 39A

| a young man | a cheap meal | a German car | a French restaurant |
| an old man | an expensive meal | an American car | an Italian restaurant |

3 What's in the pictures? Put the words in the correct order.

a	b	c	d
Italian young with ice cream an girl a	a woman expensive an car in young	man umbrella a old an black with	book Japanese newspaper a an and English

a young girl with ....

....

a black dress, black shoes

Link

➲10 **Singular and plural**

Links

nose, eyes, ears, mouth ➲26A

dress, shoes ... ➲27A

My sister is a doctor.
My brothers are students.

She's wearing a black dress.
She's wearing black shoes.

He has a large nose.
He has small eyes.

4 Complete the sentences. Write **a/an** or — (= nothing).

a John is _a_ student. His parents are _____ teachers.

b I usually wear _____ old T-shirt and _____ jeans.

c My father has _____ large ears and _____ small mouth.

d The house has _____ white walls and _____ blue door.

I'd like some bananas

Links

➲15 *some* and *any*

➲10 **Singular and plural**

Links

pen, tissues ➲40A

I'd like ... ➲77C, 34B

I'd like some bananas, please, and a pineapple.

I'd like a pen and some tissues, please.

Singular (= 1)		Plural (= 2, 3, 4, …)	
I'd like	a pineapple. a pen.	I'd like	some bananas. some tissues.

Link

need ➲54D

5 Look at this man's shopping list. Complete the sentences. Use **some** or **a/an**.

a He needs _some apples._

b He needs _____

c He needs _____

d He needs _____

e He needs _____

f He needs _____

g He needs _____

SHOPPING LIST
- apples
- T-shirt
- jeans
- eggs
- newspaper
- potatoes
- umbrella

Write in your language

My brother is a doctor.	
She has an expensive car.	
I'd like some apples, please.	

12 *the*

the, a/some; the River Nile, the Central Hotel, England, Germany …

A Grammar

Link

→11 ***a, an, some***

a melon, the melon

I'd like a melon, please,
and some oranges.

Put the melon and the
oranges in the fridge.

a melon = one melon	the melon = the melon on the table
some oranges = two, three, four … oranges	the oranges = the oranges on the table

1 Match the sentences with the pictures.

Link

Let's, Shall I, Would
you like …?   →78

a ☑2☐ Look – there's a cat.

b ☐ Where's the cat?

c ☐ Is there a car park near here?

d ☐ Drive into the car park.

e ☐ Let's buy some flowers.

f ☐ Shall I put the flowers by the window?

2 Choose the right word.

a Excuse me. Is there ⓐ / ~~the~~ good restaurant near here?

b Would you like *some* / *the* sandwiches and *a* / *the* cup of coffee?

c Where are *some* / *the* car keys? Are they in *a* / *the* living room?

d 'Where shall I put *some* / *the* eggs?'
'Put them in *a* / *the* fridge.'

e Let's go onto *a* / *the* balcony and sit down.

B Grammar

Link

is sitting   →49A

a man … the man

The picture shows a room with two people, a man

and a woman. The man is sitting in an armchair.

The woman is sitting by a piano.

1st time	2nd, 3rd, 4th … time
a man	the man
a woman	the woman
a …	the …

Room in New York, *by*
Edward Hopper (1932)

3 Fill the gaps with **a** or **the**.

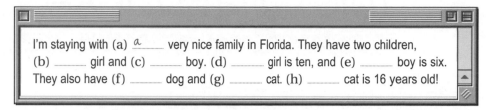

I'm staying with (a) _a_ very nice family in Florida. They have two children,
(b) _____ girl and (c) _____ boy. (d) _____ girl is ten, and (e) _____ boy is six.
They also have (f) _____ dog and (g) _____ cat. (h) _____ cat is 16 years old!

Link

living room,
bedroom ... ➔41

We're staying in (i) _____ small flat in Rome. There are three rooms:
(j) _____ living room, (k) _____ bedroom and (l) _____ kitchen.
In (m) _____ living room, there's (n) _____ big sofa and two armchairs.

C Grammar | Places

Links

north, south ... ➔37C
river, sea ➔37A
England, Germany ...
  ➔39A

the	~~the~~
the .... of ...	**Countries**
the centre of; the north/south/east/west of ...	England, Germany, Japan (but the USA)
Rivers, seas	**Cities, towns**
the River Nile, the Amazon, the Mediterranean	London, New York, Jakarta, St Petersburg
Hotels	**Streets**
the Hilton Hotel, the Embassy Hotel	New Street, 126 Kings Road, Times Square

4 Complete the sentences. Write **the** or **—** (= nothing).

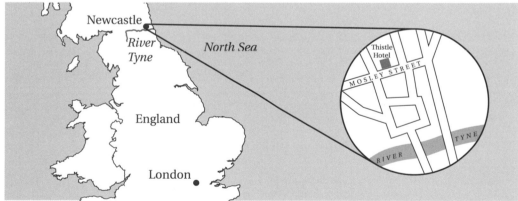

Link

in, on ➔20C

(a) _—_ Newcastle is in (b) _the_ north of (c) _____ England, about 420 km from (d) _____ London. It's on (e) _____ River Tyne and near (f) _____ North Sea.

(g) _____ Thistle Hotel is in (h) _____ Mosley Street, near (i) _____ centre of (j) _____ Newcastle. It is about 100m from (k) _____ River Tyne.

Write in your language

There's a dog in the garden.	
Put the oranges in the fridge.	
The Sun Hotel is in the centre of Tokyo.	

13 *this, that, these, those*

this/that is …, these/those are …; this/that (radio), these/those (radios); That's (nice)

A Grammar — *That's the swimming pool*

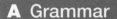

Link

→10   **Singular and plural**

Links

swimming, tennis →30
is, are   →58B

| This is the changing room … | … and these are the lockers for your clothes. | That's the swimming pool … | … and those are the tennis courts. |

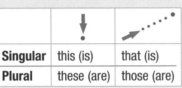

	↓	↗
Singular	this (is)	that (is)
Plural	these (are)	those (are)

EXCELSIOR
SPORTS CLUB
IT'S GOOD FOR YOU!

1 Write **this is**, **that's**, **these are** or **those are**.

a   *This is* the sauna …

b   … and _____ the showers.

c   _____ the gym …

d   … and _____ Antony – he works in the gym.

e   _____ the restaurant …

f   _____ the beauty salon …

g   … and _____ the toilets.

B Grammar — *I like this radio*

Links

I like …   →63C
Can I …?   →76C
How much …? →33C

| I like this radio. | Can I look at that guitar? | These cups are very nice. | How much are those T-shirts? |

Singular (= 1)		**Plural (= 2, 3, 4, …)**	
this / that	radio	these / those	cups

36

2 Complete the sentences. Use *this*, *that*, *these* or *those*.

a I like _that_ mirror.

b How much is _____ bowl?

c How much are _____ cushions?

d Can I look at _____ lamp?

e _____ pictures are lovely.

f Can I see _____ plates, please?

a	b	c
d	e	f

C Phrases   *That's a good idea*

Link

wonderful, interesting … ➲ 46

Are you French?

Let's go to the theatre.

Oh, I'm sorry.

I'm going to Australia in the summer.

Yes. That's right.

That's a good idea.

That's OK.

Oh, that's wonderful.

3 Write responses. Use words from the table.

a I'm reading a book about the Antarctic.
Oh, really? _That's interesting._

b We're getting married next year.
_____

c I'm sorry I'm late.
_____ Come in.

d John's very ill. He's in hospital.
Oh, _____

e Shall we go skiing at the weekend?
Yes. _____

f Are you a student at the university?
Yes. _____

That's	right.
	a good idea.
	interesting. ✓
	OK.
	wonderful.
	terrible.

Write in your language

That's the gym … and this is the sauna.	
How much are those pictures?	
'I'm sorry.' 'That's OK.'	

Countable and uncountable nouns

a book, books; money, water; a cup/bowl/glass/bottle of (water)

A Grammar

Links

➜ 11 *a, an, some*

➜ 10 **Singular and plural**

Link

bananas, apples, bread, milk ... ➜ 42

a bottle, bananas, coffee ...

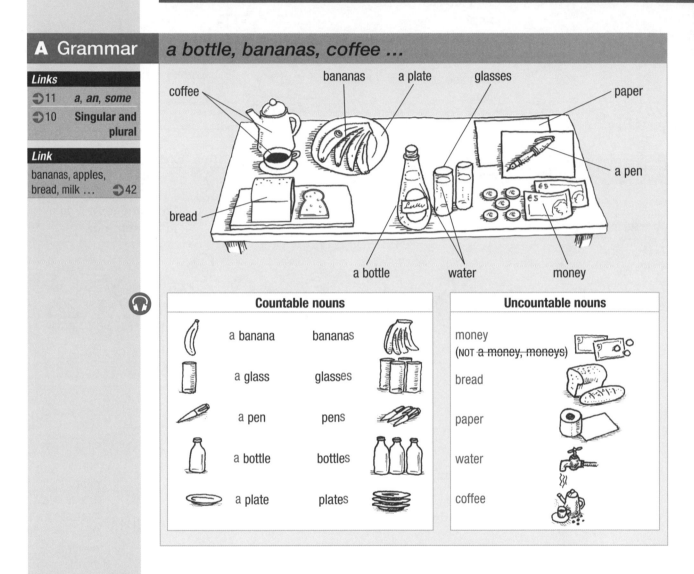

1 Countable or uncountable? Complete the table.

a clock   sugar   milk   books

apples   lemonade   a hat   hair

dogs   music   trees   grass

Countable	Uncountable
a clock	sugar
apples	

2 Choose the right word.

a They have two ☐ *dog* ✓ *dogs* and a cat.

e Do you have ☐ *milk* ☐ *a milk* in your coffee?

b Listen! I can hear ☐ *music.* ☐ *a music.*

f They're sitting on the ☐ *grass.* ☐ *grasses.*

c There's ☐ *clock* ☐ *a clock* in the bedroom.

g Can I have ☐ *apple,* ☐ *an apple,* please?

d She has long, black ☐ *hair.* ☐ *hairs.*

h Give me the ☐ *money.* ☐ *moneys.*

B Phrases

a glass of water

| water | a glass of **water** | tea | a cup of **tea** |

| rice | a bowl of **rice** | ketchup | a bottle of **ketchup** |

Would you like …?

➔78B

There's … ➔61A

some ➔15B

fridge, cupboard, table ➔41B

3 Rewrite the sentences. Use words from the table.

| a | glass cup bowl bottle | of … |

a Would you like *some soup*?
  Would you like a bowl of soup?

b Would you like *some coffee*?
  ....

c There's *some lemonade* in the fridge.
  ....

d Would you like *some orange juice*?
  ....

e There's *some olive oil* in the cupboard.
  ....

f There's *some sugar* on the table.
  ....

Write in your language

The money is on the table.	
He has red hair.	
Would you like a glass of water?	

15 *some* and *any*

a (lake), some (trees); some sugar, milk …; some (books, milk), not any (books, milk)

A Grammar

a lake, some trees

Links

→11 *a*, *an*, *some*

→10 **Singular and plural**

In the picture, you can see a lake, some trees, a mountain and some houses.

a + singular	
(You can see)	a lake. a mountain.

some + plural	
(You can see)	some trees. some houses.

mountain   trees

houses

lake

Link

bridge, tree, river …
→36

1 Write phrases with **a** or **some**.

bridge

trees

horses

people

boat

river

In the picture, you can see ⋏ river, ⋏ trees, ⋏ boat, ⋏ people, ⋏ horses and ⋏ bridge.

a _a river_   **b** _____   **c** _____

d _____   **e** _____   **f** _____

B Grammar

some milk, some sugar

Link

→14 **Countable and uncountable nouns**

Links

Can I have …?,
I'd like … →77B, C

spoon, cup, knife …
→44C

I'd like a cup of coffee, please.

Can I have some milk, please?

I'd like some sugar, please.

Can I have a spoon, please?

a + countable nouns	
(I'd like)	a cup of coffee. a spoon.

some + uncountable nouns	
(I'd like)	some milk. some sugar.

2 Choose a or some.

a Can I have ☑ *a* / ☐ *some* cigarette?

d Can I have ☐ *a* / ☐ *some* bread?

b I'd like ☐ *a* / ☐ *some* water, please.

e I'd like ☐ *a* / ☐ *some* newspaper, please.

c Can I have ☐ *a* / ☐ *some* money, please?

f I'd like ☐ *a* / ☐ *some* knife, please.

C Grammar — *some, not any*

Links

There's …, There
isn't/aren't … ➡61

clock, lamp … ➡40B

Picture A

Picture B

In Picture A …

… there's a clock.

… there's some bread.

… there are some glasses.

In Picture B …

… there isn't a clock.

… there isn't any bread.

… there aren't any glasses.

---

3 Here are more sentences about Picture B. Are they correct?
Write ✓ or correct them.

a There are some books.   There aren't any books.

b There isn't a bottle.   ✓

c There are some flowers.   ....

d There's some coffee.   ....

e There are some cushions.   ....

f There aren't any curtains.   ....

g There's a lamp.   ....

h There are some magazines.   ....

Write in your language

I'd like some flowers, please.	
Can I have some water?	
Sorry. There isn't any coffee.	

16 *a lot, much, many*

a lot, not much; a lot of / not much / not many + *noun*; How much/many …?

A Grammar

He eats a lot

Links

verb + -s, ➲63B, C
doesn't + *verb* ➲65
costs ➲33 B

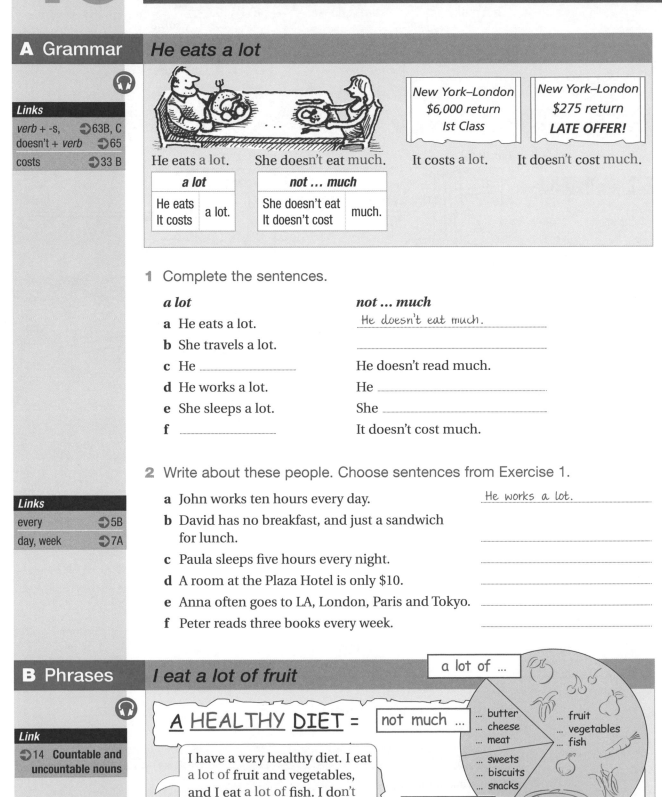

He eats a lot.   She doesn't eat much.

New York–London
$6,000 return
Ist Class

New York–London
$275 return
LATE OFFER!

It costs a lot.   It doesn't cost much.

a lot	
He eats	a lot.
It costs	

not … much	
She doesn't eat	much.
It doesn't cost	

1 Complete the sentences.

a lot

a He eats a lot.

b She travels a lot.

c He ....

d He works a lot.

e She sleeps a lot.

f ....

not … much

He doesn't eat much.

....

He doesn't read much.

He ....

She ....

It doesn't cost much.

2 Write about these people. Choose sentences from Exercise 1.

a John works ten hours every day.   He works a lot.

b David has no breakfast, and just a sandwich for lunch.

c Paula sleeps five hours every night.

d A room at the Plaza Hotel is only $10.

e Anna often goes to LA, London, Paris and Tokyo.

f Peter reads three books every week.

Links

every ➲5B
day, week ➲7A

B Phrases

I eat a lot of fruit

Link

➲14 **Countable and uncountable nouns**

A HEALTHY DIET =

a lot of …

not much …
… butter
… cheese
… meat

… fruit
… vegetables
… fish

… sweets
… biscuits
… snacks

not many …

I have a very healthy diet. I eat a lot of fruit and vegetables, and I eat a lot of fish. I don't eat much butter or cheese, and I don't eat many sweets.

Links

fruit, vegetables,
fish, butter ... ➲42

snacks, sweets,
biscuits ➲43C

I eat a lot of	fruit. fish. vegetables. sweets.

I don't eat	much	fruit. fish.
	many	vegetables. sweets.

3 Fill the gaps with **a lot of**, **much** or **many**.

1
I don't eat (a) _much_ fruit.
I eat (b) _____ meat and
(c) _____ butter. But I
don't eat (d) _____ cheese.

2
I eat (e) _____ vegetables. I
eat (f) _____ fish, but I don't
eat (g) _____ meat. I don't eat
(h) _____ sweets or biscuits.

Who has a healthy diet, **1** or **2**? _____

C Grammar

How much ...? How many ...?

Links

How ...? ➲80A
... do ...? ➲66
need ➲54D

How much **flour** do we need?

How many **eggs** do we need?

200 grams.

Four.

Californian Apple Pancakes

200 g flour

4 eggs

2 apples

500 ml milk

How much	flour milk	do we need?

How many	eggs apples	do we need?

4 Look at the cheesecake recipe. Write questions with **How much ...?** or **How many ...?**

a _How many biscuits do I need?_
Twelve.

b _____
Four.

c _____
400 grams.

d _____
75 grams.

e _____
Two.

f _____
100 grams.

ORANGE & LEMON CHEESECAKE

serves 6 people

12 biscuits
75 g butter
100 g sugar
3 lemons
4 oranges
400 g cheese
2 eggs

Write in your language

They eat a lot of vegetables ...	
... but they don't eat much fruit.	
How much cheese do we need?	

43

Pronouns (1)

I, we, you; he, she, it, they

A Grammar

I, you, we

Link

I'm, we're →58A

Singular (= 1)	Plural (= 2, 3, 4, …)
I	we
you →	you →

1 Complete the conversations. Use I, you or we.

a
How old are _you_ ?
.............'m 14.

b
Where are .... from?
............'re from Italy.

c
Are .... a teacher?
No, ...'m a doctor.

d
Hi, ...'m Ivan.
And ....'m Olga.
Hi. Are .... Russian?

B Grammar

he, she, it, they

Links

he's, she's, they're →58C

Who? What? Where? →79A

Look at these questions and answers.

Who is Gary Kasparov?
He's a chess player.

Who are Roger Federer and Lleyton Hewitt?
They're tennis players.

Where is Angkor Wat?
It's in Cambodia.

Who is Isabel Allende?
She's a writer.

What are the Urals?
They're mountains.

Gary Kasparov	Isabel Allende	Roger Federer and Lleyton Hewitt	Angkor Wat	The Urals
→ he	→ she	→ they	→ it	→ they

Singular (= 1)		Plural (= 2, 3, 4, …)	
he	😊	they	😊😊😊
she	😊	they	😊😊😊
it	☕	they	☕☕☕

2 Match the questions with the answers. Complete the answers, using words from the box.

a Who is J. K. Rowling? .... mountains.

b Where is the Colosseum? .... a film star.

c Where is Bogotá? She's a writer.

d Who is Serena Williams? .... football teams.

e Who is Russell Crowe? .... in Colombia.

f What are Juventus and Galatasaray? .... in Rome.

g What are Fuji and Kilimanjaro? .... a tennis player.

He's
She's
It's
They're

3 Look at these sentences from a letter. Make changes, using **he**, **she**, **it** or **they**.

> Hi. My name's Mario. I'm 24 years old, and I'm from Bologna, in Italy.

a   It   it
> I like Bologna. ~~Bologna~~ is a big city, but ~~Bologna~~ is very beautiful.

b My parents are teachers. ~~My parents~~ teach at the university.

c I have a brother. My brother is 15, and my brother is still at school.

d My wife's name is Lucia. Lucia is a student. Lucia studies French.

e I have a motorbike. The motorbike is very old.

f I have two sisters. My sisters live in Rome.

Links

live, teach, have, study ➲ 63A

parents, brother … ➲ 28A

Write in your language

I'm fine. How are you?	
It's a beautiful city.	
They're from Bologna.	

18 Pronouns (2)

me, us, you; him, her, them; it

A Grammar — *me, us, you*

Link

⟳17 Pronouns (1)

> I'm at home. Call me this evening.

> OK. I'll call you at 8.00.

> Come and see us at the weekend.

> OK. I'll see you on Saturday.

Subject		Object	
I	I'm at home.	me	Call me.
we	We're at home.	us	Call us.
you	You're at home.	you	I'll call you.

1 Complete these notes. Use **me**, **us** or **you**.

a Anne – I love _you_ .

b Please call _____ !
   Jack xxx

c Mary – We're at the Royal Hotel. Call _____ this evening.
   Jenny & Mark

d Hi – I'm at work. I'll call _____ later.
   C

e Pete – Thanks and goodbye! I'll see _____ at the weekend.
   F

f Please call _____ on my mobile. The number is 0884 345 81023.
   Jan

g Jim We're in town. Please meet _____ at the station at 6.
   R and E

B Grammar — *him, her, them*

Links

son, sister, parents ⟳28A

live, lives ⟳63

My son is a student. He lives at home. I see him every day.

My sister is a teacher. She lives in Paris. I see her every weekend.

My parents are very old. They live in Australia. I see them every summer.

Subject		Object	
he	He lives …	him	I see him …
she	She lives …	her	I see her …
they	They live …	them	I see them …

2 Rewrite the sentence in brackets [ ]. Use **him**, **her** or **them**.

a Maria works in London. _I see her every day._ [I see *Maria* every day.]

b Vlado is a nice boy. _____ [I like *Vlado*.]

c Where are the children? _____ [I can't see *the children*.]

d Jo and Ian are in town. _____ [I'm seeing *Jo and Ian* tonight.]

e Mr Jones lives in our street. _____ [I know *Mr Jones*.]

f There's your mother. _____ [Can you see *your mother*?]

Links

put   51B

jacket, shirt …   27A

cupboard, shelf   41B

What shall I do with your coat? — Put it in the cupboard.

What shall I do with these shirts? — Put them by the door.

Subject	Object
it	it
they	them

3 Complete the sentences. Use it or them.

What shall I do with …

a your glasses?

Put _them_ on the shelf.

b these shoes?

Put _____ by the door.

c your jacket?

Put _____ on the chair.

d this shirt?

Put _____ in the cupboard.

e your umbrella?

Put _____ on the chair.

f your trousers?

Put _____ in the cupboard.

4 Complete the sentences. Use words from the box.

Link

every   5B

| them | her | he | it | she | him | me | they |

Writer Julia Peterson talks about …

… THINGS SHE LIKES …

a My car. _It_ 's an old Volvo. I go to work in _____ every day. _____'s about 35 years old.

b My earrings. I wear _____ every day. _____'re quite cheap, but I like _____!

… AND PEOPLE SHE LIKES …

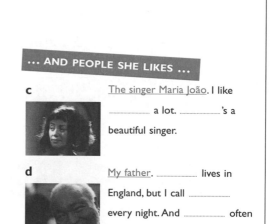

c The singer Maria João. I like _____ a lot. _____'s a beautiful singer.

d My father. _____ lives in England, but I call _____ every night. And _____ often visits _____ in New York.

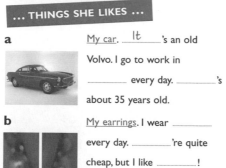

Write in your language

Come and see me on Saturday.	
I visit them every weekend.	
Paul's nice – I like him a lot.	

19 my, your, his, their ...

my, our, your; his, her, their; Kimiko's, my brother's ...

A Grammar — my, our, your

> This is my wife ...
>
> ... and this is our son.
>
> And is that your car?

| I → my : my wife | we → our : our son | you → your : your car |

Link

I, we, you ➲17A

1 Add **my**, **our** or **your**.

   a Give me *your* phone number – I'll phone you tomorrow.

   b Hello. name's Peter. What's name?

   c Here's address. Come and visit us!

   d 'I'll email you. What's email address?'

     'It's dfox@telemail.net. And mobile number is 07896 493009.'

   e We have two children. son is 18 and daughter is 16.

   f 'Excuse me – is this phone?' 'Oh, yes. Thank you.'

Link

phone number,
address ... ➲32C

B Grammar — his, her, their

Links

husband, children ...
       ➲28A

he, she, they ➲17B

AT HOME WITH LUCIA & JON

Lucia Stevenson with her husband, Jon, and their children, George and Ally. George loves his little sister!

| he → his : his brother | she → her : her husband | they → their : their children |

2 Write **his**, **her** or **their**.

On other pages

a	Michael Schumacher and _his_ new Ferrari	*page* **14**
b	Bill and Hillary Clinton in _____ Californian villa	**19**
c	Mariah Carey talks about _____ new song	**23**
d	David Beckham at home with _____ family	**25**
e	SPECIAL! Catherine and Michael with _____ baby daughter	**28**
f	Mick Jagger on _____ 60th birthday	**33**

C Grammar — *Kimiko's family*

Link

Japanese, French, the USA … ➲39A

Kimiko's husband is French.
Her husband's name is Michel.
Michel's father is a film star.

AN INTERNATIONAL FAMILY

Kimiko is Japanese, but her husband Michel is French. Michel is the son of film star Paul Leblanc. They live in a large house in Nice.

3 Complete the sentences. Use words from the box, and add **'s**.

Kimiko	Her brother
Nina	Ami

'I have a sister, Ami, and a brother, Izo,' says Kimiko. 'My sister is married to a German doctor. They live in Frankfurt.

'My brother lives in the USA. He has a house in Chicago. He isn't married, but he has a girlfriend called Nina. Her father is Italian, but her mother is Brazilian.'

a _Kimiko's_ sister is married.

b _____ husband is German.

c _____ brother lives in the USA.

d _____ name is Izo.

e _____ house is in Chicago.

f _____ mother is Brazilian.

Write in your language

Here's my mobile number.	
This is our daughter, Joanna.	
George's wife is Brazilian.	

20 Place prepositions (1)

in, on, under, over, by

A Phrases

in, on, under, over

Link
door, wall ➔41C

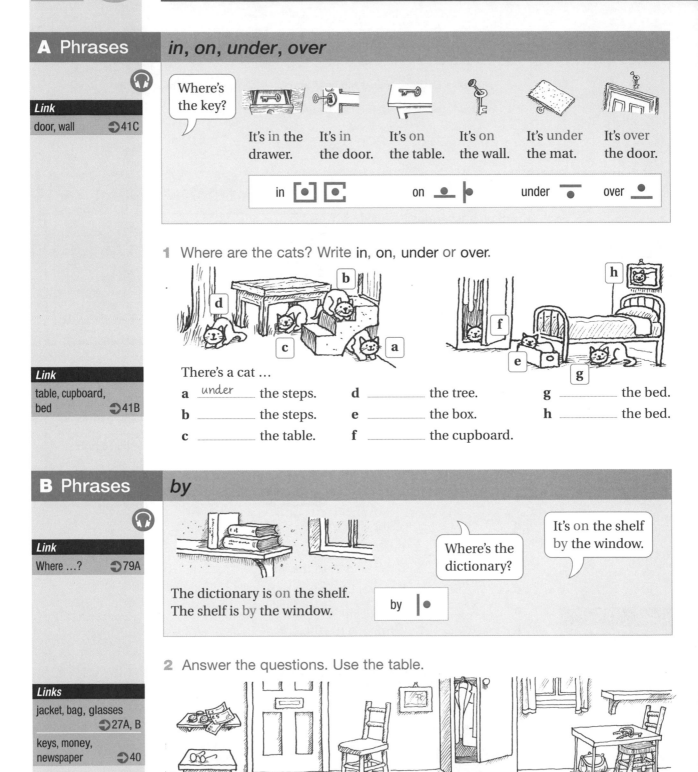

Where's the key?

It's in the drawer. It's in the door. It's on the table. It's on the wall. It's under the mat. It's over the door.

| in | ⊡ ◧ | on | ●⎮◗ | under | ⊤ | over | ●⎯ |

1 Where are the cats? Write **in, on, under** or **over**.

Link
table, cupboard, bed ➔41B

There's a cat …

a	under the steps.	d	the tree.	g	the bed.
b	the steps.	e	the box.	h	the bed.
c	the table.	f	the cupboard.		

B Phrases

by

Link
Where …? ➔79A

The dictionary is on the shelf.
The shelf is by the window.

Where's the dictionary?

It's on the shelf by the window.

| by | ⎮● |

2 Answer the questions. Use the table.

Links
jacket, bag, glasses ➔27A, B

keys, money, newspaper ➔40

a Where's my bag?
b Where's my jacket?
c Where are my glasses?

d Where are my keys?
e Where's my newspaper?
f Where's my money?

on		
in	…	by …
under		

Link

it's, they're ➲17B

a It's under the table by the window .

b It's ....

c They're ....

d They're ....

e It's ....

f It's ....

C Phrases

in the centre, on a river

Link

in the north of ...,
on the coast ➲37

Liverpool

M62

River Mersey

Hotels

5
3
1
4
2

It's easy to get to ...

Liverpool is in the north of England, on the River Mersey.

It's on the railway line from London, and it's on the M62 motorway.

Where to stay ...

1 Adelphi Hotel ****
In the city centre.

2 Moat House Hotel ****
In a quiet suburb.

3 Thistle Hotel ***
On the edge of the city.

4 Village Hotel, Whiston ***
In the country, 30 km from Liverpool.

5 Spa Hotel, Southport ****
On the coast, 25 km from Liverpool.

in ⬭   on ⟋

in	England Liverpool

in	the centre a suburb the country

on	a river a road a motorway a railway line the coast

on the edge of ...

3 Complete the sentences with **in** or **on**. Match them with the places.

Link

Egypt, Russia, Brazil ...
➲39A

a [4] It's on the edge of Cairo, in Egypt.

b ☐ It's .... Russia, ... the Trans-Siberian Railway.

c ☐ It's .... Brazil, ... the coast.

d ☐ It's .... the River Ganges, ... India.

e ☐ It's .... Greece, ... the centre of Athens.

f ☐ It's .... the Mississippi River, ... the USA.

1 New Orleans
2 Calcutta
3 The Acropolis
4 The Great Pyramid
5 Omsk
6 Rio de Janeiro

Write in your language

Your bag's on the chair by the window.	
Is your village on the railway line?	
They live on the edge of the city.	

21 Place prepositions (2)

next to, beside, in front of, behind, between; near, opposite; above, below

A Phrases

next to, between ...

Look at this photo of the Smith family in 2002.

John is standing next to (OR beside) Leon.

Leon is standing between John and Clara.

John is standing behind Emma.

Emma is standing in front of John.

John   Leon   Clara

Emma

Links

| stand, sit | ➲49A |
| is ...-ing | ➲69A |

1 Look at this photo of the Smith family in 1920 and the text below. Write the names of the people.

a ....

b ....

c ....

d ....

e ....

f ....

g ....

h ....

i John

j ....

Daniel is sitting on the table beside John.
Lily is standing between Nat and George.
Frieda is holding John's hand.
William is standing next to Frieda.
David is sitting in front of William.

George is standing behind John.
Victoria is sitting in front of Lily.
Victoria is sitting between Daniel and Albert.

2 Complete the sentences.

a Albert _is sitting next to_ .... Victoria.

b Lily .... Daniel.

c Nat .... Lily.

d John .... Daniel and Frieda.

e William .... David.

B Phrases — *next to, near, opposite*

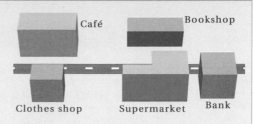

The bank is next to the supermarket.
There's a bookshop opposite the supermarket.
The clothes shop is near the supermarket.
There's a café near the supermarket.

Café   Bookshop

Clothes shop   Supermarket   Bank

3 Look at the map and answer the questions. Use **next to**, **near** or **opposite**.

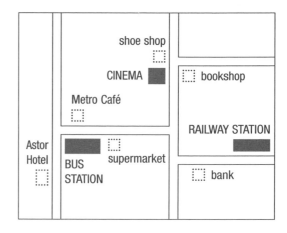

shoe shop
CINEMA
Metro Café
Astor Hotel
BUS STATION
supermarket
bookshop
RAILWAY STATION
bank

a Where's the supermarket?

It's next to the bus station.

b Where's the bank?

_____

c Where's the Metro Café?

_____

d Where's the bookshop?

_____

e Where's the shoe shop?

_____

f Where's the Astor Hotel?

_____

Links

bus station, bank …
➲35A

bookshop,
clothes shop … ➲34A

Where …?
➲35B, 79A

C Phrases — *above, below*

The plane is flying above the clouds.   The plane is flying below the clouds.

4 Complete the sentences. Use **above** or **below**.

1	Real Madrid	9 points
2	Man United	7 points
3	Inter Milan	6 points

a Manchester United are *below* Real Madrid in the table.

b The temperature in Munich is 3° _____ zero.

c Manchester United are _____ Inter Milan.

d Lake Ontario is 90 metres _____ Lake Eyrie.

e Lake Eyrie is 90 metres _____ Lake Ontario.

f The temperature in Moscow is 5° _____ zero.

g Mr Smith's flat is _____ an office.

Lake Eyrie 540m
Lake Ontario 450m

3	John Smith
2	TEXCO Inc.
1	TEXCO Inc.

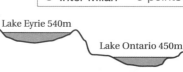

Moscow	−5°C
Munich	3°C
Nairobi	12°C

Write in your language

There's a café opposite the bookshop.	
They're standing in front of the café.	
My flat's near the station.	

22 *at* and *to*

at (the airport), to (the airport); at home/work/school; go home, go to work/school

A Phrases — *at the station*

Link

station, cinema ...
⊃35A

I'm at the station. I'm at a party. We're at the Excelsior Hotel.

at	the station	at	the cinema	at	a football match
	the airport		the swimming pool		a party
	the bus stop				a hotel

1 Where are these people? Use phrases from the box above.

a She's at the airport.

b They're _____

c He's _____

d She's _____

e They're _____

f They're _____

a

b

c

d

e

f

B Phrases — *at the airport, to the airport*

Links

go to ... ⊃50C

(I'm) ...-ing ⊃68, 70

She's going to the airport.   She's at the airport.

2 Add **at** or **to**.

            to

a What time are you going the party?

b They're staying the Astor Hotel.

c I'm standing the bus stop.

d Are you going the football match?

e There's a café the station.

f I'm going the airport now.

at work, to work

Links

works for	➲ 29B
at 12.00	➲ 4B
in the evening, afternoon …	➲ 5C

Max Green works for a radio station. He goes to work at 12.00 and goes home at 10.00 in the evening.

His daughter, Teresa, goes to school at 8.00 and goes home at 2.00.
Max doesn't see Teresa much. When she's at home, he's at work; and when he's at home, she's at school.

He/She …	
… is at school.	… goes to school.
… is at work.	… goes to work.
… is at home.	… goes home.
	❗ NOT ~~to home~~.

3 Are these sentences correct? Write ✓ or correct them.

a Max goes to work at 8.00. *Max goes to work at 12.00.*
b Teresa goes to school at 8.00. ✓
c Teresa is at home in the afternoon.
d Max is at home in the afternoon.
e Teresa is at home in the morning.
f Teresa goes home at 2.00.
g Max goes to school at 12.00.

4 Answer the questions. Write sentences with **at** or **to**.

Link

Where? What time?
➲ 79A, B

a What time do you go to work or school? *I go*
b What time do you go home?
c Where are you at 8.00 in the evening? *I'm*
d Where are you at 10.00 in the morning?

Write in your language

We're staying at a hotel.	
He's not at home – he's at work.	
What time are you going home?	

A Phrases

into, out of, onto, off

Links

put, take	51B
cupboard, fridge, shelf	41B

Put the chicken in the oven.

Take the chicken out of the oven.

Put the book on the shelf.

Take the book off the shelf.

in OR into →☐	out of ←☐	on OR onto ⌒	off ⟋

1 Complete the sentences, using **in**, **out of**, **on** or **off**.
Match the two parts of each sentence.

a Take the pizza _out of_ the box ...   ... and put it _____ the shelf.

b Take your clothes _____ the bed ...   ... and put it _in_ the oven.

c Take the milk _____ the car ...   ... and put them _____ a plate.

d Take that book _____ the chair ...   ... and put them _____ the cupboard.

e Take the plates _____ the cupboard ...   ... and put it _____ the fridge.

f Take the potatoes _____ the oven ...   ... and put them _____ the table.

2 Where does the cat go?
Write **into**, **onto**, **out of** or **off**.

a _into_ the room   **e** _____ the bed

b _____ the cupboard   **f** _____ the table

c _____ the cupboard   **g** _____ the house

d _____ the bed   **h** _____ the garden

B Phrases

along the road, under the bridge ...

Link

24   **Giving directions**

To get to the park, you go ...

1 along the road

2 under the bridge

3 up the steps

4 over the bridge

5 down the steps

6 across the main road

7 through the gates

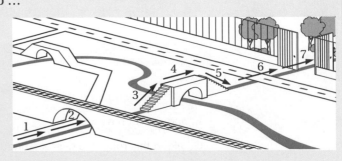

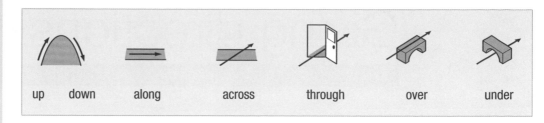

up	down	along	across	through	over	under

3 Choose the right word.

Go (a) ☑ *across* / ☐ *along* the street, (b) ☐ *across* / ☐ *through* a gate,

(c) ☐ *up* / ☐ *down* some steps and (d) ☐ *under* / ☐ *through* a door.

Go (e) ☐ *along* / ☐ *down* the hill, (f) ☐ *across* / ☐ *along* a river,

(g) ☐ *along* / ☐ *over* a road and (h) ☐ *across* / ☐ *along* the field.

Go (i) ☐ *down* / ☐ *across* the car park, (j) ☐ *down* / ☐ *across* some

steps, (k) ☐ *under* / ☐ *along* a road and (l) ☐ *under* / ☐ *along* a bridge.

4 Match the signs with the sentences. Complete the sentences.

a [5] You can go out _through_ this door.
b ☐ Go _____ the stairs to the office.
c ☐ It costs 75¢ to drive _____ the bridge.
d ☐ Go _____ the stairs to the toilet.
e ☐ You can't ride your bike _____ this path.
f ☐ Turn on your lights when you go _____ the tunnel.
g ☐ The bus can't go _____ that bridge.

1 TOILETS
2 1500m
3 (no bikes)

4 OFFICE 1ST FLOOR
5 EXIT
6 Low Bridge 4.4 m 14'-6"
7 **Toll Bridge** Bikes 25¢ Cars 75¢ Buses €2.00

Write in your language

Take the pizza out of the oven …	
… and put it on a plate.	
Go along this road and over the bridge.	

Link

gate, hill, river …
➲ 36A

24 Giving directions

go down/along this road; go straight on; turn left/right (at); go past

A Phrases

Go along this road and turn left

Link

➲72   **Imperatives**

Links

Can you …?   ➲77A
How …?   ➲80A
get to   ➲31C
station, bank,
cinema …   ➲35A
along   ➲23B

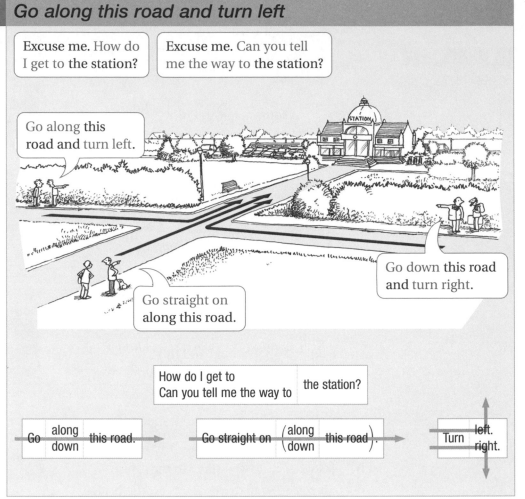

Excuse me. How do I get to the station?

Excuse me. Can you tell me the way to the station?

Go along this road and turn left.

Go down this road and turn right.

Go straight on along this road.

| How do I get to | the station? |
| Can you tell me the way to | |

| Go | along | this road. |
| | down | |

| Go straight on | (along | this road). |
| | (down | |

| Turn | left. |
| | right. |

---

1 Read the directions. Complete the questions.

a How do I get to _the swimming pool_ ?
Go along this road, then turn right and go straight on.

b Can you tell me _____ ?
Go down this road and turn left. Then turn right and go straight on.

c How do I _____ ?
Go along this road and turn right. Then turn right again and go straight on.

d Can _____ ?
Go down this road and turn left. Then turn left again and go straight on.

e How _____ ?
Go along this road and turn right. Then turn left and go straight on.

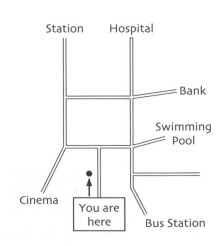

Station   Hospital

Bank

Swimming Pool

Cinema

You are here

Bus Station

2 Complete the answers.

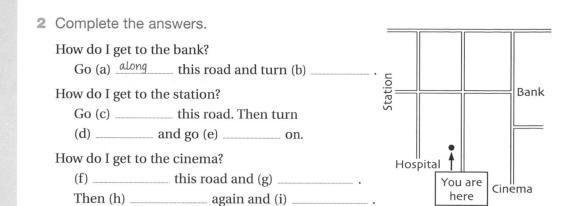

How do I get to the bank?

Go (a) _along_ this road and turn (b) _____ .

How do I get to the station?

Go (c) _____ this road. Then turn

(d) _____ and go (e) _____ on.

How do I get to the cinema?

(f) _____ this road and (g) _____ .

Then (h) _____ again and (i) _____ .

B Phrases

Link

at   ⮕22A

Turn left at the café

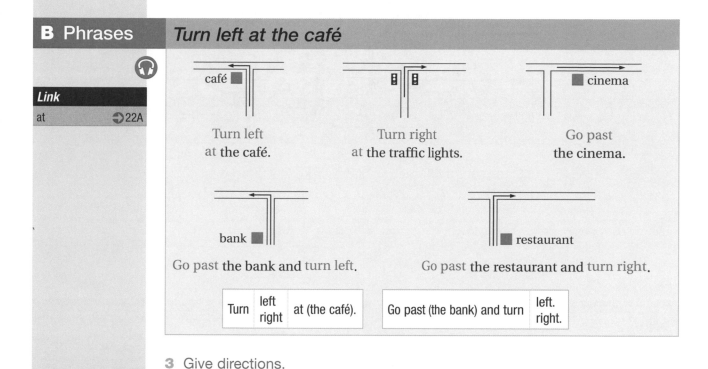

Turn left
at the café.

Turn right
at the traffic lights.

Go past
the cinema.

Go past **the bank and** turn left.

Go past **the restaurant and** turn right.

Turn	left right	at (the café).

Go past (the bank) and turn	left. right.

3 Give directions.

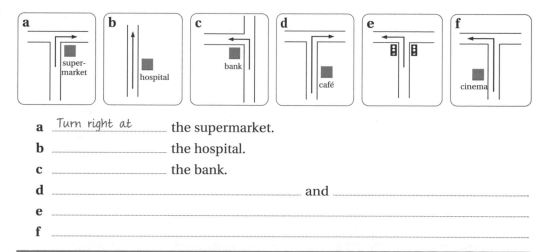

a | b | c | d | e | f
super-market | hospital | bank | café | | cinema

a _Turn right at_ the supermarket.

b _____ the hospital.

c _____ the bank.

d _____ and _____

e _____

f _____

Write in your language

Can you tell me the way to the bank?	
Go straight along this road.	
Go past the hotel and turn right.	

People

man, woman, baby ...; tall/short; short, brown hair, blue eyes ...; (a boy) with (glasses)

A Vocabulary — *man, woman ...*

teenager

baby

man

girl

boy

woman

1 Complete the table.

♂	♀	Age:
man		20+
		13–19
		3–12
		0–2

B Phrases — *She's very short*

Look at the identity cards.

Links

very, quite	➔ 45B
has	➔ 56A
green, blue ...	➔ 47A

Name: ANNA LOMAX
Height: 1m 50
Hair: brown
Eyes: green

Name: JOHN DUNN
Height: 1m 98
Hair: fair
Eyes: blue

Name: ELENA ROSSI
Height: 1m 74
Hair: black
Eyes: brown

Name: JUAN PEREZ
Height: 1m 65
Hair: grey
Eyes: brown

Anna Lomax is very short. She has short, brown hair and green eyes.

John Dunn is very tall. He has fair hair and blue eyes.

Elena Rossi is quite tall. She has long, black hair and brown eyes.

Juan Perez is quite short. He has grey hair and brown eyes.

2 Complete the tables.

a

He	is	very	short.
She		quite	

b

He	has	short	brown	hair.
She				

c

He	has	green	eyes.
She			

3 Write about these people.

a Amy McLeod is _quite tall_ .
She has _____ and
_____ .

b Jon Dean _____
_____
_____ .

Now write about you.

I'm _____ . I have _____
and _____ .

Name: AMY McLEOD
Height: 1m 72
Hair: fair
Eyes: green

Name: JON DEAN
Height: 1m 65
Hair: black
Eyes: brown

C Phrases

a boy with glasses

a woman + long hair
= a woman with long hair

a boy + glasses
= a boy with glasses

a man + a beard
= a man with a beard

a woman		long hair
a boy	with	glasses
a man		a beard

4 Put the words in the correct order. Find the six people in the picture.

a man long with a hair fair
☐9 _a man with long, fair hair_

b dog with a a girl
☐ _____

c black with woman hair long a
☐ _____

d a with beard man a long
☐ _____

e umbrella with an man a
☐ _____

f old glasses an with woman
☐ _____

Link
a, an ➲11

Write in your language

Is your baby a boy or a girl?	
He has dark hair and blue eyes.	
He's a tall man with glasses.	

26 The body

face, eyes, nose, mouth …; large/small (ears), a long/round face; arms, legs, feet, tail …

A Vocabulary   The face

Link

⊙72   **Imperatives**

How to draw a cartoon

Arnold Schwarzenegger

1 Draw the head.

2 Draw the hair.

3 Draw the ears.

4 Draw the eyes.

5 Draw the nose.

6 Draw the mouth.

1 Complete the instructions.

Mick Jagger

a Draw the head.

b Draw the

c Draw the

d Draw the

e Draw the

f Draw the

B Phrases   *a long, thin face*

Links

long, short (hair) ⊙25B
large, small   ⊙45A
has   ⊙56A

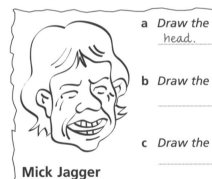

Ed Brown has a long, thin face. He has small eyes, a small nose, small ears and a small mouth.

Rita Brown has a round face. She has large eyes, a large nose, large ears and a large mouth.

a	round	face
	long, thin	

a	small	mouth
	large	nose

small	eyes
large	ears

62

2 Write about the two children.

a Sam Brown has _a round face_ . He has ____,
____ , ____ and ____ .

b Sara Brown has ____ . She has ____,
____ , ____ and ____ .

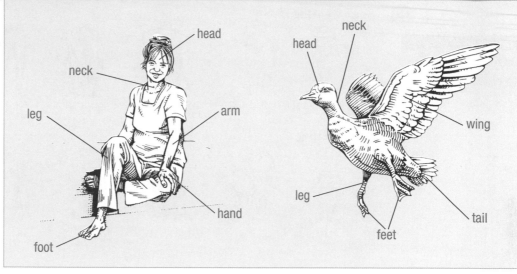

3 Write the parts of the body.

a _tail_   **f** ____
b ____   **g** ____
c ____   **h** ____
d ____   **i** ____
e ____   **j** ____

4 Match the sentences with the pictures.

a [4] It has four legs and a tail.
b [ ] It has a tail, but no legs or feet.
c [ ] It has eight legs, but no wings.
d [ ] It has wings and six legs.
e [ ] It has wings, two legs and a tail.
f [ ] It has two arms, two legs and two feet, but no tail.

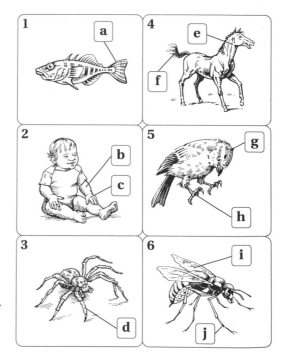

Link

two, four, six, eight
➔1A

Write in your language

He has long hair and large eyes.	
It has a long tail.	
They have six legs and four wings.	

27 Clothes

dress, shirt, trousers …; wear, carry; put on, take off; get dressed/undressed

A Vocabulary | *They're wearing …*

Link
He's/She's …-ing
➔69A

She's wearing …

| a dress | a skirt | a top | a coat | jeans | a hat |

He's wearing …

| a suit | a shirt | a jacket | trousers | a T-shirt | a jumper |

❗ jeans, trousers, NOT ~~a jeans, a trousers~~

1 What are they wearing?

| a | b | c | d | e | f | g |

a He's wearing _a suit_ .
b She's wearing _____ .
c She's wearing _____ and _____ .
d He's wearing _____ and _____ .
e He's wearing _____ and _____ .
f She's wearing _____ and _____ .
g He's wearing _____ and _____ .

B Vocabulary | *wear, carry*

Link
a, an ➔11

You wear …

| a coat | shoes | glasses | a tie | wear a coat |

You carry …

| an umbrella | a bag | a suitcase | a baby | carry a coat |

2 Write sentences with **wearing** or **carrying**. Use words from the box.

a He's wearing a suit.

　 He's _____

b She's _____

　 _____

c _____

　 _____

d _____

bag	coat	dress	glasses
✓ suit	suitcase	umbrella	

a b c d

C Phrases

put on, take off ...

Link

put, take ➲51B

put on a coat	take off a coat	get dressed	get undressed
You're cold → you put on your coat	You're hot → you take off your coat	get dressed = put on your clothes	get undressed = take off your clothes

Links

cold, warm,
It's raining ➲38

I'm hot, ill ➲48D

3 Choose the right verb.

a It's cold today. ☑ *Put on* / ☐ *Take off* some warm clothes.

b ☐ *Put on* / ☐ *Take off* your shoes. They're dirty.

c It's 8 o'clock. Let's ☐ *get dressed* / ☐ *get undressed* and have breakfast.

d I'm hot. I think I'll ☐ *put on* / ☐ *take off* my jacket.

e I feel tired. I think I'll ☐ *get dressed* / ☐ *get undressed* and go to bed.

f It's raining. ☐ *Put on* / ☐ *Take off* your coat.

Write in your language

He's wearing a jacket and trousers.	
Put on some warm clothes.	
Take off your coat.	

28 The family

mother, father, daughter …; is/isn't married; has (two sisters), doesn't have any (children)

A Vocabulary | Parents and children

Tsar Nicholas II of Russia and his family in 1914

Tatiana · Olga · Maria · Alexandra · Alexei · Nicholas · Anastasia

father …

… and son

mother …

… and daughter

parents …

… and children

husband …

… and wife

brother …

… and sister

1 Choose the right word.

a Alexei is Maria's ~~son~~ / (brother) / ~~father~~ .

b Alexandra and Nicholas are Anastasia's *parents / children* .

c Nicholas is Alexei's *son / brother / father* .

d Alexandra is Nicholas's *wife / daughter / sister* .

e Anastasia is Alexandra's *mother / sister / daughter* .

Now complete the sentences.

f Nicholas is Alexandra's _husband_ .

g Maria is Nicholas's _____ .

h Alexei is Nicholas's _____ .

i Anastasia is Alexei's _____ .

j Alexandra is Maria's _____ .

k Olga is Tatiana's _____ .

2 Complete the table.

♂	♀
father	mother
son	
	sister
	wife

Link

…'s → 19C

She's married

 Look at this family tree.

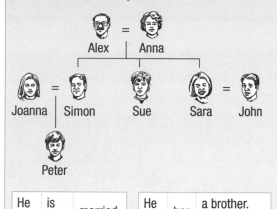

Anna is married. She has three children: Simon, Sue and Sara.

Simon is married, and he has one child.

Sara is married, but she doesn't have any children.

Sue isn't married.

Peter doesn't have any brothers or sisters.

Links

is, isn't ⮑ 59B

has, doesn't have ⮑ 56B, 65A

any ⮑ 15C

He She	is isn't	married.

He She	has	a brother. two children.

He She	doesn't have	any children. any brothers or sisters.

3 Find the people in this family tree. Write the numbers.

a ☐11 Ali doesn't have any brothers or sisters.

b ☐ Mark is married and has three children.

c ☐ Paula isn't married. She has a sister and a brother.

d ☐ Leo has a sister. He isn't married.

e ☐ Dimitri has two children.

f ☐ Elisabeth has a brother, and she's married. She doesn't have any sisters.

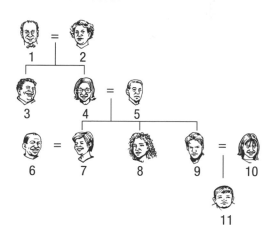

4 Look at the examples. Write about you.

....

....

....

....

....

I'm married.

I have three children.

I don't have any brothers or sisters.

I'm not married.

Links

I'm, I'm not ⮑ 59A

have, don't have ⮑ 56A, 64A

Write in your language

I have a sister and two brothers.	
My daughter isn't married.	
They don't have any children.	

29 Work

secretary, shop assistant ...; work in, work for; What do you do?, Where do you work?

A Vocabulary | Places and jobs

Link

hotel, restaurant ...
➲ 35A

an office   a hotel   a restaurant

a hospital   a shop   a school

Links

He's ..., She's ...
➲ 58C

works ➲ 63C

1 Look at the people. Complete the sentences.

a She's a secretary. She <u>works in an office.</u>

b He's a waiter. He <u>works in a restaurant.</u>

c He's a receptionist.
He _____

d She's a teacher. She _____

e She's a nurse. She _____

f He's a shop assistant.
He _____

g She's a waitress. She _____

h He's a doctor. He _____

a	secretary	e	nurse
b	waiter	f	shop assistant
c	receptionist	g	waitress
d	teacher	h	doctor

2 Look at the signs. Write the jobs from Exercise 1.

a <u>secretary</u>

b _____ , _____

c _____

d _____ , _____

e _____

f _____

a **OFFICE**

b **BANGKOK** Thai Restaurant

c **PARK HOTEL** ▶

d ✚ **St Peter's Hospital**

e 📚 **FULLERS** The Bookshop

f **HILL ROAD** Secondary School

work for

George is a taxi driver.
He works for City Taxis.

Olivia works in an office.
She works for Hi-Tec Computers.

George and Olivia
work for companies.

George works for a
taxi company.

Olivia works for a
computer company.

3 Write about these people.

a She works in a bank.   She works for O'Doherty's Bank.

b He's a French teacher.

c She works in a bookshop.

d He's a receptionist in a hotel.

e She's a waitress.

f He works in a supermarket.

SaveCo
·············
There's a SaveCo
Supermarket near you!

GOURMETS
The best restaurant in town

O'DOHERTY'S BANK
Your money is our business

Plaza International
☆☆☆☆
HOTELS IN 50 COUNTRIES

*Learn French, Spanish, German,
Italian or Japanese with*
LANGUAGE DIRECT

BOOKS • BOOKS • BOOKS
BAILEYS
BOOKS • BOOKS • BOOKS

What do you do?

Link
Where do you …?,
What do you …?
➔66C

What do you do?   I'm a nurse.   I work for Alpha Taxis.

Where do you work?   I work in a bank.

4 Complete the questions and answers.

a ' Where do you _____ work?' ' I work in a _____ shop.'

b '_____ do?' '_____ Gourmets.'

c 'Where _____ .' '_____ a restaurant.'

d 'What _____ ?' '_____ teacher.'

Write in your language

She works in a hospital. She's a doctor.	
What do you do?	
I work for Plaza International.	

30 Sport and leisure

football, tennis, golf …; play, watch; go + -ing ; play the (piano), play (cards)

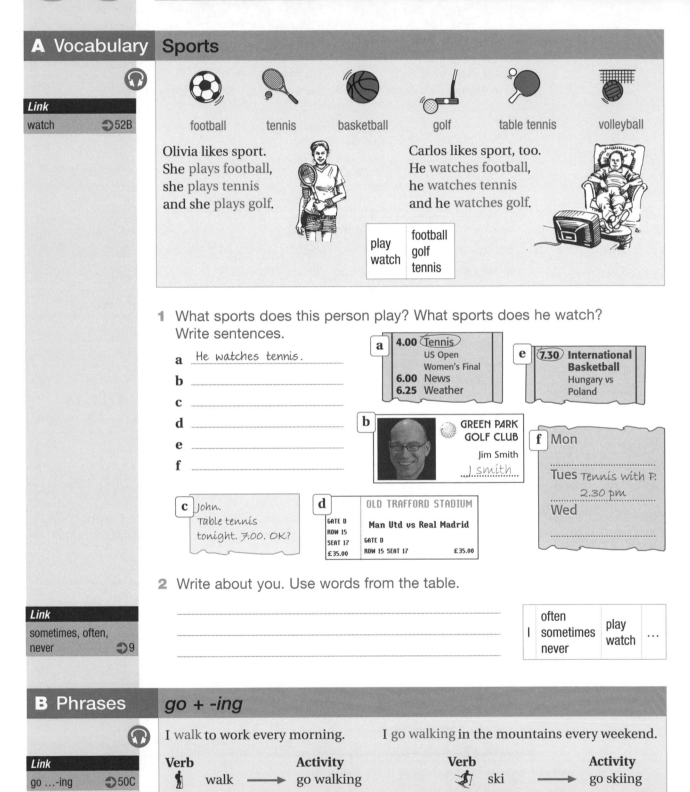

A Vocabulary | Sports

Link

watch ⮕52B

football tennis basketball golf table tennis volleyball

Olivia likes sport.
She plays football,
she plays tennis
and she plays golf.

Carlos likes sport, too.
He watches football,
he watches tennis
and he watches golf.

play watch	football golf tennis

1 What sports does this person play? What sports does he watch?
Write sentences.

a He watches tennis.
b
c
d
e
f

a 4.00 Tennis
US Open
Women's Final
6.00 News
6.25 Weather

e 7.30 International Basketball
Hungary vs Poland

b GREEN PARK GOLF CLUB
Jim Smith
J. Smith

f Mon
Tues Tennis with P.
2.30 pm
Wed

c John.
Table tennis
tonight. 7.00. OK?

d OLD TRAFFORD STADIUM
GATE D
ROW 15
SEAT 17
£35.00
Man Utd vs Real Madrid
GATE D
ROW 15 SEAT 17   £35.00

2 Write about you. Use words from the table.

Link

sometimes, often,
never ⮕9

I	often sometimes never	play watch	…

B Phrases | go + -ing

Link

go …-ing ⮕50C

I walk to work every morning.   I go walking in the mountains every weekend.

Verb		Activity	Verb		Activity
🚶	walk	→ go walking	🎿	ski	→ go skiing
🏃	run	→ go running	🎣	fish	→ go fishing
🏊	swim	→ go swimming	💃	dance	→ go dancing

3 When do you wear these things on your feet?
Complete the sentences.

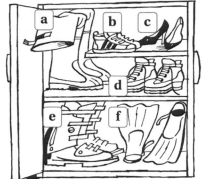

a You wear these _when you go fishing._
b You wear these _when you_
c You wear these
d You wear these
e You wear these
f You wear these

Link

wear   ➲ 27

C Phrases   *play the piano, play cards*

He's playing   She's playing   They're playing   They're playing   She's playing a
the piano.   the guitar.   cards.   chess.   computer game.

play	the piano the guitar

play	cards chess a computer game

4 Read about four sisters – Angie, Bella, Clara and Diana.

Link

don't, doesn't ➲ 64, 65

Clara plays the guitar, but Angie, Bella and Diana don't.
Diana doesn't play the piano.
Bella often plays chess with Clara.
Diana often plays cards with Angie.
Bella plays computer games, but Angie, Clara and
Diana don't.
The girl in the picture doesn't play chess.

Who is the girl in the picture?

Write sentences about her. Use **She plays …** or **She doesn't play …**

a _She plays the piano._   **d**
b   **e**
c

Write in your language

I play tennis, but I don't play golf.	
They often go fishing.	
He plays the guitar.	

31 Transport

in a car/taxi; on a bus, train, plane …; go by (bus); leave, arrive in/get to

A Vocabulary — *on a train*

Link

in, on ➲20A

a bus

a train

a tram

a car

a motorbike

a plane

a bike

a boat

a taxi

| in | a car |
| | a taxi |

on	a bus
	a tram
	a train
	a bike
	a motorbike
	a boat
	a plane

1 Where are these people?

a They're *on a tram.*

b He's _____

c They're _____

d He's _____

e They're _____

f She's _____

a

b

c

d

e

f

B Phrases — *I go by bus*

Links

go ➲50

walk ➲49C

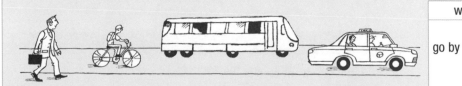

	walk
go by	bus
	bike
	car
	…

Some people walk **to work.** Some people go by bike. Some people go by bus. But I go by taxi.

2 How do these people go to work? Complete the sentences.

a He _goes by train._

b She _goes_ _____

c He _____

d She _____

e She _____

f He _____

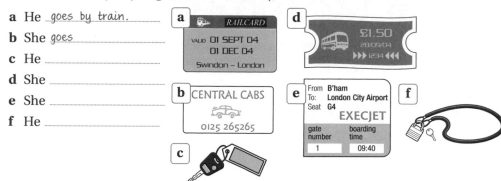
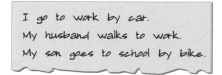

Link

verb + -s ➲ 63C

3 Look at the examples. Write about you and your family.

_I go_ _____

_My_ _____

_____

_____

> I go to work by car.
> My husband walks to work.
> My son goes to school by bike.

Links

go to work, school ➲ 22C

husband, son ➲ 28A

C Vocabulary Leaving and arriving

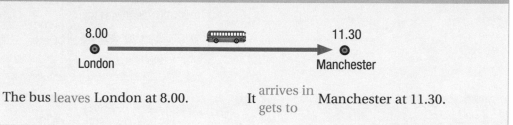

The bus leaves London at 8.00.   It arrives in / gets to Manchester at 11.30.

Links

at 11.30 ➲ 4B

on Sunday ➲ 5A

4 Look at the timetables and complete the sentences. Use **leaves** or **arrives in / gets to**.

a The bus _arrives in_ London at 8.30.

b The plane _____ New York at 7.00.

c The boat _____ Singapore at 6.00 on Wednesday.

d The bus _____ Oxford at 6.30.

e The train _____ Paris at 11.45.

f The boat _____ Jakarta at 8.00 on Tuesday.

g The train _____ Marseille at 4.45.

h The plane _____ Miami at 10.30.

> Oxford 6.30
> London 8.30

Your flight to Miami:
New York (JFK) ➡ Miami Int.
07.00   10.30

| Jakarta | 8:00 | Tues |
| Singapore | 6:00 | Wed |

Paris   11.45
Lyon   ↓
Marseille 4.45

Write in your language

He goes to work by car.	
The plane leaves London at 8.00.	
It arrives in Paris at 10.00.	

Communicating

letter, fax, email, text message; (fax) them / send them (a fax); computer, printer ...

A Vocabulary — *letter, fax ...*

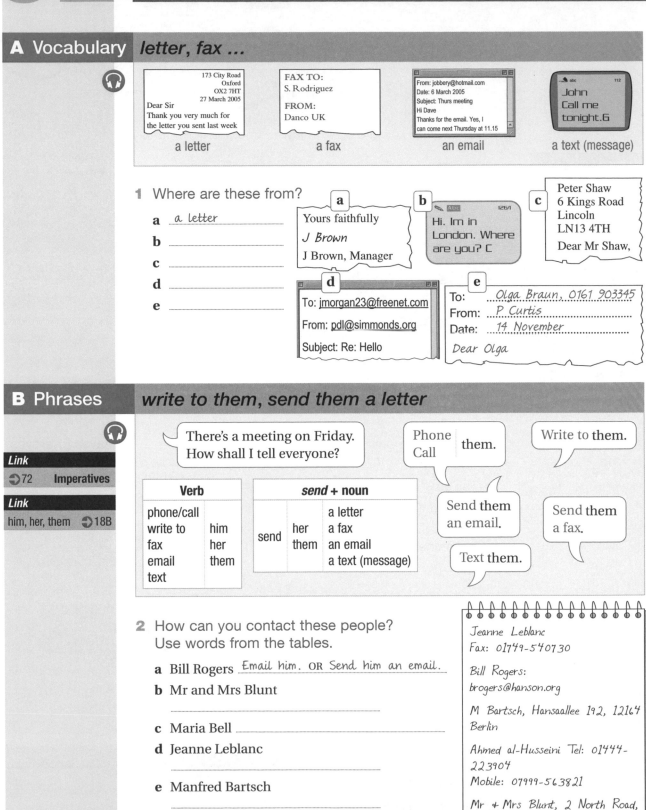

173 City Road Oxford OX2 7HT 27 March 2005 Dear Sir Thank you very much for the letter you sent last week	FAX TO: S. Rodriguez FROM: Danco UK	From: jobbery@hotmail.com Date: 6 March 2005 Subject: Thurs meeting Hi Dave Thanks for the email. Yes, I can come next Thursday at 11.15	abc 112 John Call me tonight.6
a letter	a fax	an email	a text (message)

1 Where are these from?

a   a letter

b   ....

c   ....

d   ....

e   ....

a
Yours faithfully
J Brown
J Brown, Manager

b
Abc   126/1
Hi. Im in
London. Where
are you? C

c
Peter Shaw
6 Kings Road
Lincoln
LN13 4TH
Dear Mr Shaw,

d
To: jmorgan23@freenet.com
From: pdl@simmonds.org
Subject: Re: Hello

e
To: *Olga Braun, 0161 903345*
From: *P Curtis*
Date: *14 November*
Dear Olga

B Phrases — *write to them, send them a letter*

Link
→ 72   Imperatives

Link
him, her, them → 18B

There's a meeting on Friday.
How shall I tell everyone?

Phone / Call   them.

Write to **them**.

Verb			*send* + noun		
phone/call write to fax email text	him her them		send	her them	a letter a fax an email a text (message)

Send **them** an email.

Text **them**.

Send **them** a fax.

2 How can you contact these people?
Use words from the tables.

a Bill Rogers   *Email him.* OR *Send him an email.*

b Mr and Mrs Blunt

   ....

c Maria Bell   ....

d Jeanne Leblanc

   ....

e Manfred Bartsch

   ....

f Ahmed al-Husseini

   ....

Jeanne Leblanc
Fax: 01749-540730

Bill Rogers:
brogers@hanson.org

M Bartsch, Hansaallee 192, 12164
Berlin

Ahmed al-Husseini Tel: 01444-
223904
Mobile: 07999-563821

Mr + Mrs Blunt, 2 North Road,
Chelmsford, Essex CH6 5BT

MARIA BELL   mbell@exnet.com

address, phone number ...

Link

...'s 　　　➲19C

Sophie Brown's address

Name: Sophie Brown

125 London Road,
Brighton BR11 9WT, UK

sbrown44@telemail.net

her phone number

☎ 01273 8849001

📠 01273 8849035 — *her* fax number

📱 06771 935 003

her email address

her mobile number

3 Look at Exercises 1 and 2. Complete the sentences.

a Ahmed al-Husseini's *phone number* is 01444-223904.

b John Morgan's _____ is jmorgan23@freenet.com.

c Manfred Bartsch's _____ is Hansaallee 192, 12164 Berlin.

d Peter Shaw's _____ is 6, Kings Road, Lincoln LN13 4TH.

e Ahmed al-Husseini's _____ is 07999-563821.

f Jeanne Leblanc's _____ is 01749-540730.

Can I use your fax machine?

Link

➲40 　　**Things**

Link

Can I ...? 　　➲76C

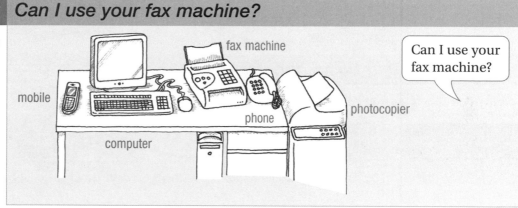

fax machine

mobile

phone

photocopier

computer

Can I use your fax machine?

4 You're in a friend's office. Ask questions.

a You want to copy a letter. 　　*Can I use your photocopier?*

b You want to send a fax.

c You want to write an email.

d You want to copy some pictures.

e You want to talk to your mother.

f You want to send a text message.

Write in your language

Send them an email.	
Can I use your phone?	
What's your mobile number?	

33 Money

one (euro) fifty; It costs …; How much is it / does it cost?; He/She earns…

A Vocabulary — *nine pounds ninety-nine*

Link
➊ 1 Numbers (1)

one	dollar	twenty-five
	euro	fifty
	pound	ninety-nine

two	dollars	twenty-five
nine	euros	fifty
	pounds	ninety-nine

one euro fifty

two dollars twenty-five

nine pounds ninety-nine

1 How much are these things?

a six euros seventy-five

b ....

c ....

d ....

e ....

f ....

a €6·75
b U.S.Postage $1·40
c £14·99
d €4·50
e $3·20
f £1·85

B Phrases — *It costs about $15*

Link
about ➊ 8B

In the USA …

$240 $255 $251

… a TV costs about $250.

$9,100 $9,200 $8,800

… a small car costs about $9,000.

2 Complete the sentences about the USA. Use **about**.

a A mobile phone costs about seventy dollars.

b A CD ....

c A printer ....

d A pair of jeans ....

e A good mountain bike ....

f A cheap camera ....

COLORMATIC CAMERA
$41.50

RELAY–X
MOUNTAIN BIKE
$610

COLOUR
PRINTER
JS10455X
$99.00

CDs **$9.99**

BULLIT Jeans $49.95

XY Mobile phone
$69.50

3 Write sentences about your country.

In my country …

… a TV costs about .... … a pair of jeans ....

… a CD .... … a small car ....

How much does it cost?

Link

⇒34   **Shops and shopping**

Links

How much …? ⇒80A
do, does   ⇒66, 67
this, these   ⇒13B

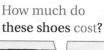

"How much is this book?"

"How much do these shoes cost?"

| How much | is this book? |
| | are these shoes? |

| How much | does this book | cost? |
| | do these shoes | |

4 Write questions. Use **How much is/are …?** or **How much do/does … cost?**

a   How much does this radio cost?   **a** radio

b _____   **d** shirt

c _____   **e** camera

d _____

e _____

f _____

b sunglasses   **c** bag   **f** trainers

She earns €150,000 a year

Links

day, week, month, year   ⇒7A
doctor, waiter, secretary …   ⇒29A

She's a doctor. She earns €150,000 a year.

He's a waiter. He earns €80 a day.

| He She | earns … | a day. a week. a month. a year. |

5 Write about these people. Use the numbers in brackets [ ].

a She   earns €3,500 a month.   [€3,500]

b He _____ [€72,000]

c She _____ [€750]

d He _____ [€100]

e She _____ [€1,800]

f He _____ [€48,000]

a SECRETARY
€42,000 a year

b UNIVERSITY TEACHER
€6,000 a month

c NURSE
€39,000 a year

d SHOP ASSISTANT
€600 a week
MON-SAT

e WAITRESS
€450 a week

f TAXI DRIVER
€4,000 a month

Write in your language

This phone costs $49.50.	
How much is this watch?	
She earns €25,000 a month.	

34 Shops and shopping

butcher, chemist, bookshop …; buy, sell; Can I have / I'd like …; open/closed

Link
➲ 35   **Towns**

Links
at   ➲ 22A
You can …   ➲ 76A

Links
meat, bread, cakes
    ➲ 42, 43
clothes, shoes   ➲ 27
newspaper,
magazines   ➲ 40B

Link
go shopping   ➲ 50C

A Vocabulary Shops

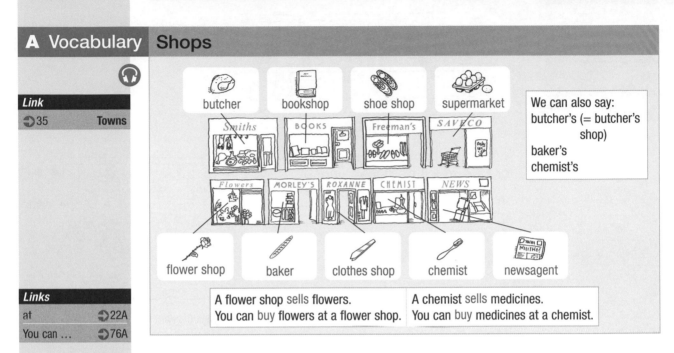

We can also say:
butcher's (= butcher's shop)
baker's
chemist's

A flower shop sells flowers.
You can buy flowers at a flower shop.

A chemist sells medicines.
You can buy medicines at a chemist.

1 Write answers 1–8 in the diagram.

1 You can buy meat at a _____ . ▶
2 You can buy clothes at a _____ . ▶
3 You can buy flowers at a _____ . ▶
4 A _____ sells bread and cakes. ▶
5 A _____ sells newspapers. ▶
6 You can buy medicines at a _____ . ▶
7 A _____ sells shoes. ▶
8 A _____ sells meat, bread, magazines … ▶

Now complete the sentence:
9▼ You can buy this book at a _____ .

2 Where do you go? Draw lines on the map.

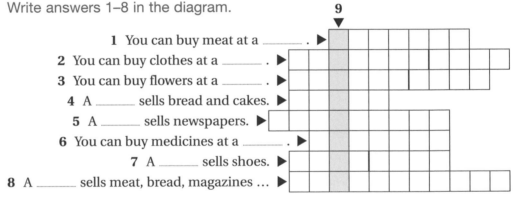

You go shopping. You buy …

(1)  a chicken,
(2) a newspaper,
(3) a toothbrush,
(4) a dictionary,
(5) a baguette,
(6) a tie,
(7) a pair of trainers and (8) a rose.

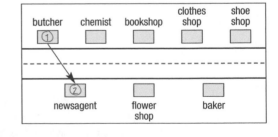

Buying things

Links

I'd like … ⟳54C

Can I have …? ⟳76C

bananas, eggs,
potatoes … ⟳42

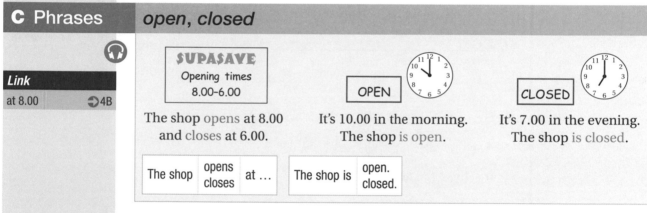

> I'd like four bananas, please.

> That's €1.60.

> Can I have a kilo of potatoes, please?

> Yes, certainly.

3 Look at the shopping list and complete the questions.
Use **I'd like …** or **Can I have …?**

a ___Can I have six eggs, please?___

Yes – large or small?

b _____

How many would you like?

c _____

Sorry. We don't sell bread.

d _____

This one is two kilos. Is that OK?

e _____

What colour – red, yellow or white?

f _____

Yes – strawberry or chocolate?

> Shopping list
>
> some apples   a large chicken
>
> 6 roses   an ice cream
>
> 6 eggs   a baguette

open, closed

Link

at 8.00   ⟳4B

SUPASAVE
Opening times
8.00–6.00

OPEN

CLOSED

The shop opens at 8.00 and closes at 6.00.

It's 10.00 in the morning. The shop is open.

It's 7.00 in the evening. The shop is closed.

| The shop | opens closes | at … |

| The shop is | open. closed. |

4 Complete the sentences.

Link

Saturday, Sunday …
    ⟳5A

a On Saturday, the bookshop ___opens___ at 9.00.

b The bookshop isn't _____ on Sunday.

c The restaurant is _____ on Sunday evening.

d On Saturday, the restaurant _____ at 12.00.

e The restaurant is _____ on Monday.

f On Wednesday, the bookshop _____ at 7.00.

STONES BOOKSHOP	
Mon–Fri	8.00–7.00
Saturday	9.00–4.00
Sunday	Closed

PIZZARAMA RESTAURANT	
Monday	Closed
Tues–Fri	12.00–10.00
Saturday	12.00–11.30
Sunday	4.00–10.00

Write in your language

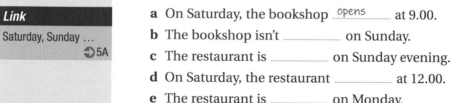

I'd like a chicken, please.	
The newsagent opens at 6.30.	
The library is closed on Sunday.	

post office, cinema, hotel …; Where's the (library)?; stairs, lift, garage …

A Vocabulary Places in towns

Link

⟹34   **Shops and shopping**

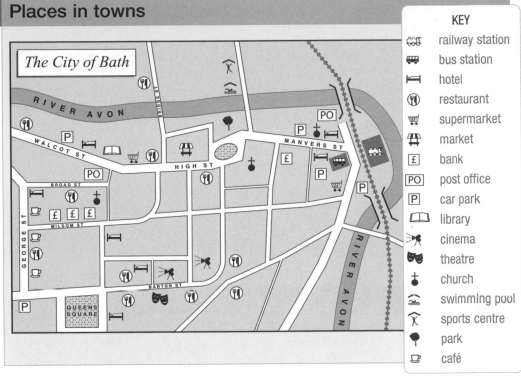

KEY

🚂	railway station
🚌	bus station
🛏	hotel
🍴	restaurant
🛒	supermarket
♨	market
£	bank
PO	post office
P	car park
📖	library
✖	cinema
🎭	theatre
✝	church
⚓	swimming pool
🏹	sports centre
🌳	park
☕	café

1 Read the tourist information. What are the places?

a For food shopping, try the big ___supermarket___ in Walcot Street.

b There are three _____ in Milsom Street.

c The last train to London leaves the _____ at 10.38.

d The _____, in Walcot Street, has about 28,000 books.

e There are some good _____ in George Street.

f There are four _____ in Barton Street.

g The _____ has tennis, volleyball and basketball.

2 Where can you see these signs?

Link

at   ⟹22 A

a _at a bus station_

b _at a_ _____

c _____

d _____

e _____

f _____

a BUSES TO LONDON Wait here ↓

b Rooms 101–129 →

c

d CARS

0–1 hour	1.50
1–2 hours	3.00
2–4 hours	5.00

e PARCELS HERE

f TONIGHT'S FILMS

1 STAR WARS 1	16.00	20.30
2 RIVER OF LOVE	17.00	20.00

Where is it?

Links

Where …?   ➲79A

next to, opposite ➲21B

Where's the hotel?

It's …
… in **Walcot Street**.
… next to **the library**.
… opposite **the post office**.

Where's the hotel?

It's …
… at the end of **Broad Street**.
… at the corner of **George Street and Broad Street**.

3 Look at the map in A. Write questions with **Where's …?**

a *Where's the swimming pool?*   It's next to the sports centre.

b _____   It's opposite the railway station.

c _____   It's at the end of Broad Street, opposite a church.

d _____   It's in Barton Street, opposite the theatre.

e _____   It's at the corner of Walcot Street and Bridge Street.

f _____   It's in Manvers Street, next to the car park.

C Vocabulary Buildings in towns

Link

➲2   Numbers (2)

Link

floor   ➲2B

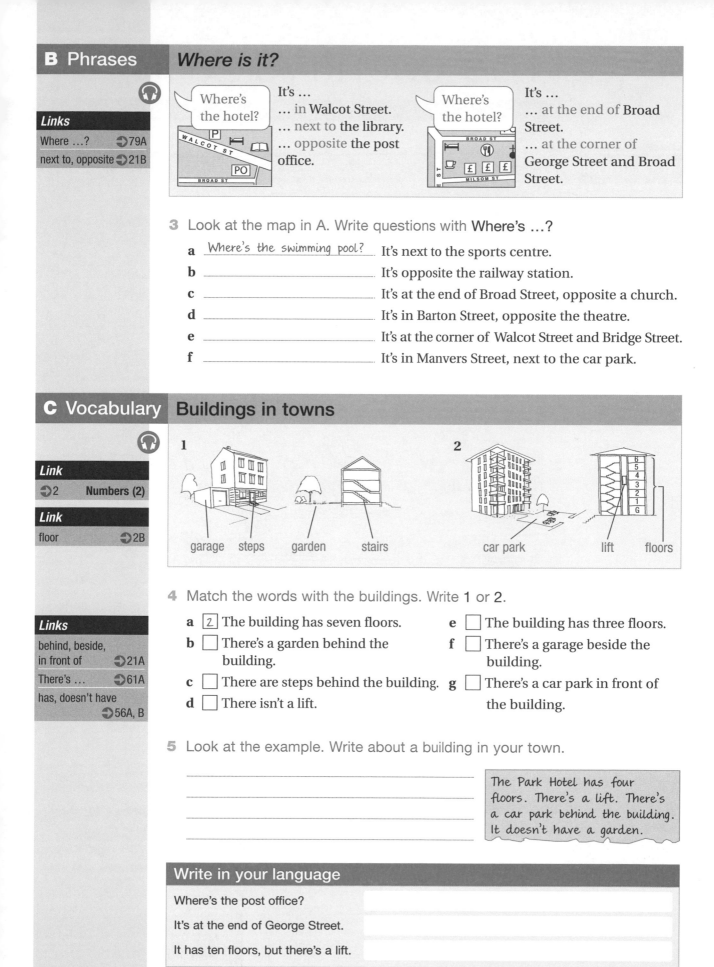

1   garage   steps   garden   stairs

2   car park   lift   floors

Links

behind, beside,
in front of   ➲21A

There's …   ➲61A

has, doesn't have
        ➲56A, B

4 Match the words with the buildings. Write **1** or **2**.

a [2] The building has seven floors.

b [ ] There's a garden behind the building.

c [ ] There are steps behind the building.

d [ ] There isn't a lift.

e [ ] The building has three floors.

f [ ] There's a garage beside the building.

g [ ] There's a car park in front of the building.

5 Look at the example. Write about a building in your town.

_____

_____

_____

_____

The Park Hotel has four floors. There's a lift. There's a car park behind the building. It doesn't have a garden.

Write in your language

Where's the post office?

It's at the end of George Street.

It has ten floors, but there's a lift.

36 The countryside

field, fence, path, gate ...; grass, tree, flower; horse, cow, sheep ...

A Vocabulary | In the countryside

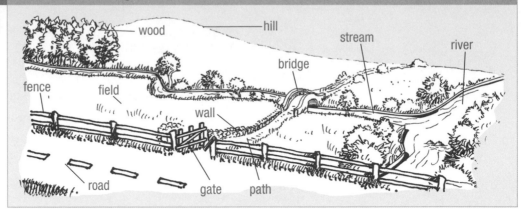

1 Read the directions. Where is the person going?

a Go through the gate, along a wall, through another gate, past a wood, over a stream and up a hill.

Answer: _____

b Go along the road, over a bridge, through a gate, along a fence and up a hill.

Answer: _____

c Go through the gate, over a wall, across a field, over a stream and through a wood.

Answer: _____

Links

through, along, over ...	⮌ 23B
past	⮌ 24C

2 Where does the path go? Write the phrases in the correct order.

up the hill	through the wood
across the field	along the fence
through the gate	✓across the bridge

It goes ...

a _across the bridge_

b _____

c _____

d _____

e _____

f _____

tree

cat

horse

sheep

flowers

cow

bird

grass

dog

Links

is + ...-ing	➲69A
There is/are ...	➲61A
on, under, by	➲20A, B

3 Complete the sentences.

In the picture ...

a there's a _cat_ on the wall.

b there are three _____s.

c there's a _____ by the gate.

d a _____ is eating _____ .

e there's a _____ on the fence.

f a _____ is drinking water.

g there are some _____s under the _____ .

Links

this, these	➲13A
wings, legs	➲26C

4 Find 15 answers in the wordsquare. Write the words.

a You can walk along these: _road_
path

b This has wings and two legs: _____

c These can go round a field: _____

d This goes over a river or a road: _____

e You can swim in these: _____

f These have four legs: _____

g You see these in the garden: _____ _____ _____

```
C O U G R A S S B
T R E E I S N H R
B I R D V T T E I
F L O W E R S E D
E R A A R E Y P G
N C D L P A T H E
C O S L I M D O G
E W D H O R S E E
```

Now look at the *other* letters in the wordsquare, and complete the sentence:

You can see all of these things in the _ _ _ _ _ _ _ _ _ _ _ .

Write in your language

The path goes through a wood.	
There's a bridge over the stream.	
There are some cows in the field.	

37 Natural features

mountain, forest, river ...; on (a river), in (the mountains); in the (north) of

A Vocabulary — *mountains, lakes, forests ...*

Link
→36 **The countryside**

hills
the sea
an island
a river
a beach
mountains
a lake
a forest

1 Complete the sentences. Use words from the box.

> beaches   forests   ✓ hills   islands   lakes   mountains   rivers   sea

VIETNAM   a   b   c

Caribbean   d   e   f   g   h   **Switzerland**

Vietnam – a beautiful country of (a) _hills_, (b) _____ and (c) _____ .

Come to the Caribbean for beautiful (d) _____, sunny (e) _____ and blue (f) _____ .

Visit our (g) _____ and swim in our (h) _____ .

Link
sunny, warm →38B, C

Links
a lot of, not many →16B
There are/aren't ... →61A, B

2 Look at the examples about England. Write two sentences about your country.

In _____ , there are _____

There aren't _____

> In England, there are a lot of beaches.
> There aren't many mountains or forests.

B Phrases — *on, in*

Link
on, in →20A

London — River Thames

Brazil — Rio de Janeiro

Lake Geneva — Geneva

Kathmandu

London is on a river.

Rio de Janeiro is on the sea. / on the coast.

Geneva is on a lake.

Kathmandu is in the mountains.

on	a river		on	the sea		in	the mountains
	a lake			the coast			

3 Look at the map. Answer the questions.

Link

Is ...? ⮕ 60B

a Is Quito on the coast?
   No. It's in the mountains.

b Is Guayaquil in the mountains?

c Is Lima on a lake?

d Is Puno on the sea?

e Is Iquitos on a lake?

f Is Cuzco on the coast?

C Phrases *north, south, east, west*

Bilbao is in the north of Spain.
Granada is in the south of Spain.
Madrid is in the centre of Spain.
Salamanca is in the west of Spain.
Valencia is in the east of Spain.

4 Complete the sentences. Use expressions from the table.

a

	north	
	south	
in the	east	of ...
	west	
	centre	

I live in Nice. It's
in the south of
France.

b

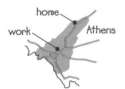

Maria lives ....
Athens. She works ....
.... Athens.

Link

live, lives ⮕ 63

c

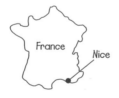

We're staying ....
.... Italy.

d

My uncle lives ....
.... Scotland.

e

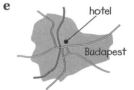

Our hotel is ....
.... Budapest.

Write in your language

We live on the coast.	
They're staying in the mountains.	
Bristol is in the west of England.	

38 Weather

beautiful/nice/terrible …; hot, warm, cold …; sun, wind, rain, snow; It's raining/snowing

A Phrases

It's lovely!

Links

What's … like? ➔79B

good, bad, lovely …
➔46

very, quite ➔45B

What's the weather like?

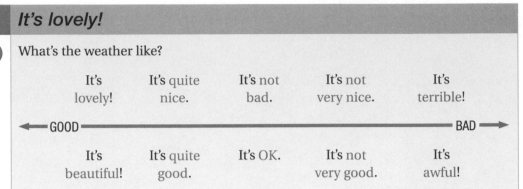

It's lovely!	It's quite nice.	It's not bad.	It's not very nice.	It's terrible!

⟵ GOOD ——————————————————————— BAD ⟶

It's beautiful!	It's quite good.	It's OK.	It's not very good.	It's awful!

1 Write the missing words in the crossword.

1 😊 The weather's _ _ _ _ _ _ _ _ _ today.

2 'Is the weather good?'
    ☹ 'No, it's _ _ _ _ _ !'

3 'What's the weather like?'
    😐 'It's not _ _ _ .'

4 ☹ The weather here is _ _ _ _ _ _ _ _ _ .

5 'What's the _ _ _ _ _ _ _ like?'

6 😊 'It's _ _ _ _ _ good.'

7 😐 The weather's not very _ _ _ _ today.

8 😊 It's a _ _ _ _ _ _ day today!

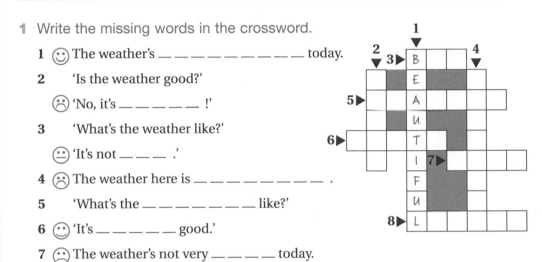

B Phrases

It's hot

Link

hot, cold ➔45A

very hot	40°
hot	30°
warm	20°
cool	10°
cold	0°
very cold	–10°

Dubai	30°	Rome	19°
Kuala Lumpur	39°	São Paulo	28°
London	9°	Tokyo	11°
Moscow	–12°	Warsaw	2°

2 Complete the sentences.

a It's hot _____ in Dubai.
b _____ in Kuala Lumpur.
c _____ in London.
d _____ in Moscow.

e _____ in Rome.
f _____ in São Paulo.
g _____ in Tokyo.
h _____ in Warsaw.

It's sunny

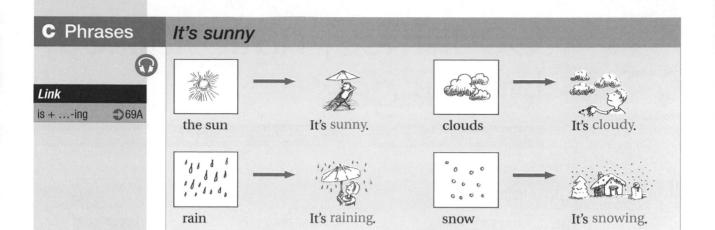

the sun → It's sunny.   clouds → It's cloudy.

rain → It's raining.   snow → It's snowing.

3 Look at the map. Complete the sentences.

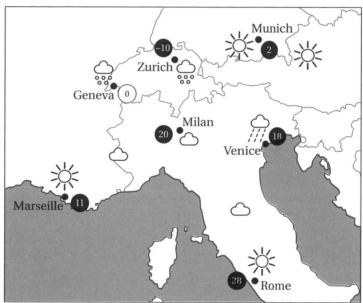

a In Zurich, *it's very cold and it's snowing.*

b In Munich, _____

c In Venice, _____

d In Geneva, _____

e In Rome, _____

f In Milan, _____

g In Marseille, _____

Write in your language

What's the weather like?	
It's lovely. It's warm and it's sunny.	
It's terrible. It's cold and it's raining.	

39

Countries, nationalities, languages

She's from (France, Egypt …); She's (French, Egyptian …); She speaks (French, Arabic …)

A Vocabulary · *He's American*

Link

he's, she's, we're …
⮕58

David Bowie is
English/British.
He's from England/Britain.

Tiger Woods is
American.
He's from the USA.

Juliette Binoche
is French.
She's from France.

1 Read about these people. Complete the table.

He's/She's …	He's/She's from …
English	England
British	Britain
American	the USA
French	France
	Japan
German	
	Italy
Chinese	
	Russia
Spanish	
	Brazil
Egyptian	

GERMANY Berlin

Steffi Graf is
from Germany.

JAPAN Tokyo

Yoyo Ma is
Japanese.

BRAZIL
Brasília

Ronaldo is
Brazilian.

RUSSIA
Moscow

Vladimir Putin
is Russian.

SPAIN
Madrid

Penélope Cruz
is from Spain.

Jackie Chan is
from China.

Umberto Eco
is Italian.

Mona Zaki is
from Egypt.

CHINA
Beijing

ITALY
Rome

EGYPT Cairo

2 Write the sentences in a different way.

a I'm *from England.*
I'm English.

b We're *French.*

c Are you *Russian?*

d His wife is *from Brazil.*

e She's *from Italy.*

f They're *from the USA.*

g Are they *British?*

h He isn't *from China.* He's *from Japan.*

3 Look at these sentences from magazines. Write the correct countries and nationalities.

Japan

a He works in Tokyo, the capital of ~~China~~.

d Michael Schuhmacher, the Chinese racing driver

b She drives a British car – a Citroën.

e *I love Spanish food: pizza, spaghetti, tortelloni,*

c The River Nile, in Brazil, is 6,750 km

f She enjoys German music, especially Tchaikovsky

B Phrases

They speak English

Hello!	Bonjour!	Guten Tag!	Ciao!	Holá!
English	'Hello' in French	'Hello' in German	'Hello' in Italian	'Hello' in Spanish

Здра́вствуйте	السلام عليكم	你好	こんにちは
'Hello' in Russian	'Hello' in Arabic	'Hello' in Chinese	'Hello' in Japanese

---

4 Write answers 2–9 in the diagram.

10 ▼

1 In Rome and Napoli, people speak … ► I T A L I A N

2 In Tokyo and Osaka, people speak … ►

3 In Beijing and Shanghai, people speak … ►

4 In Berlin, Frankfurt and Vienna, people speak … ►

5 In Moscow and St Petersburg, people speak … ►

6 In Cairo, Riyadh and Dubai, people speak … ►

7 In Sydney and New York, people speak … ►

8 In Paris and Marseille, people speak … ►

9 In Madrid and Buenos Aires, ► people speak …

Now complete the sentence:

10▼ There are nine _____ in this exercise.

---

5 Look at the examples. Write about you and your country.

In _____

In school, _____

I _____

> In England, people speak English.
> At school, people learn French and German. I speak French and Spanish, but I don't speak German.

Write in your language

Are you American?	
I don't speak Arabic.	
She's from China.	

Link

I speak / don't speak
⮕ 64A

40 Things

key, make-up, credit card ...; plant, mirror, clock ...

A Vocabulary Personal things

Link

phone, mobile ➤32D

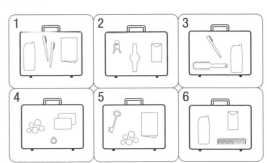

money
keys
a brush
a watch
a pen

a phone OR mobile (phone)
a credit card
a ring
a comb
a passport
tissues

1 Match the words with the X-ray pictures.

a ☐6 a phone, tissues and a comb
b ☐ a phone, a pen and a brush
c ☐ a key, a passport and money
d ☐ a phone, pens and a passport
e ☐ money, credit cards and a ring
f ☐ keys, a watch and tissues

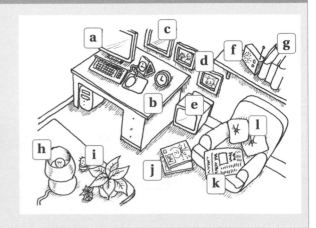

2 What do you need?

Link

want, need ➤54A, D

a You want to phone a friend. _a phone_
b You want to open a door. _____
c You want to go to the UK. _____
d You want to write a postcard. _____

e You want to know the time. _____
f You want to buy a coat. _____ OR _____

B Vocabulary Things in rooms

Links

desk, shelf, wall, floor ... ➤41
There is/are ... ➤61A
in, on ➤20A
a, some ➤11D

There are lots of things in my room. On the table, there's a lamp and some plants, and on the shelf, there are some books and a radio. On the desk, there's a computer and two clocks.

There are two cushions and a newspaper on the armchair. On the wall, there are two pictures and a mirror. And there's a television and some magazines on the floor.

3 What are the things in the picture opposite?

a	a computer	**d**		**g**		**j**	
b	clocks	**e**		**h**		**k**	
c		**f**		**i**		**l**	

4 Look at the two pictures. Write the words.

Picture A

Picture B

			A	B
a	a plant		There's one on the floor.	There's one on the shelf.
b			There are three.	There are two.
c			There's one on the wall.	There isn't one on the wall.
d			There are six.	There are three.
e			There's one on the shelf.	There's one on the table.
f			There's one on the table.	There's one on the chair.
g			There's one on the shelf.	There's one on the shelf.

5 Find 14 answers in the wordsquare. Write the words.

Links

You can …	➔76A
these	➔13A

a You can buy things with these: money

b You can read these:

c You can write letters with these:

d Two parts of a room:

e You can wear these:

f Two things for your hair:

g You can sit on these:

```
C  R  E  D  I  T  C  A  R  D
U  N  E  W  S  P  A  P  E  R
S  C  O  M  P  U  T  E  R  P
H  C  W  O  X  R  I  N  G  B
I  O  A  N  W  A  T  C  H  R
O  M  L  E  C  H  A  I  R  U
N  B  L  Y  F  L  O  O  R  S
Y  M  A  G  A  Z  I  N  E  H
```

Write in your language

You need some money and a passport.	
There's a phone on the desk.	
Where are my keys?	

A Vocabulary   Rooms

Link
There is/are … ➲61A

This flat has five rooms.

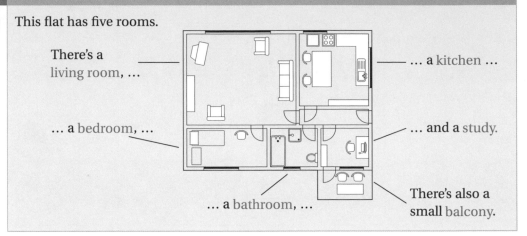

There's a
living room, …

… a kitchen …

… a bedroom, …

… and a study.

… a bathroom, …

There's also a
small balcony.

1 Which rooms are these?

 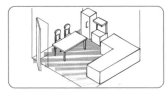 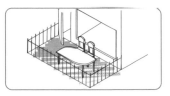

a _This is the study._   **b** _This is the_   **c** _____

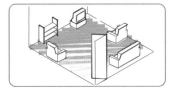 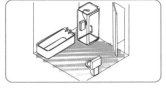 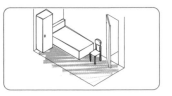

d _____   **e** _____   **f** _____

B Vocabulary   Furniture

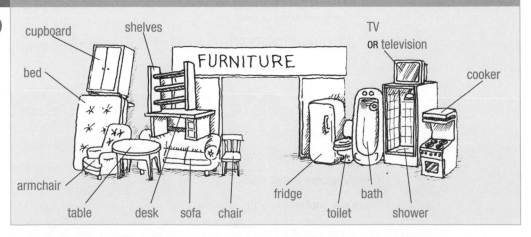

cupboard   shelves   TV
OR television

bed   cooker

FURNITURE

armchair   fridge   bath

table   desk   sofa   chair   toilet   shower

2 Look at the rooms in Exercise 1. What is in them? Complete the lists.

in the study	in the kitchen	in the living room	in the bathroom	in the bedroom	on the balcony
shelves	a cooker	armchairs			
a chair					

C Phrases

on the wall, in the corner …

Links

in, on, by   ➜ 20A, B

picture, table, cushions …   ➜ 40B

There's a desk by the window.

There's a picture on the wall.

corner

There's a TV in the corner.

wall

window

door

There's a table by the door.

There are some cushions on the floor.

floor

3 In this room …

a There's a mirror _on the wall._

b There's a table _____

c There's a chair _____

d There's a clock _____

e There's a cupboard _____

f There's a TV _____

4 Look at the example. Write about a room in your house or flat.

In my _____
_____
_____
_____

> In my bedroom, there's a bed, a table and a cupboard. There are some shelves on the wall, and there's a chair by the window.

Write in your language

My flat has two bedrooms.	
There's a desk in the study.	
There's a cupboard by the window.	

42 Food and drink (1)

meat, fish, eggs, bread …; coffee, milk, water …; *fruit & vegetables*; a kilo/litre of …

A Vocabulary — Food and drink

Link

➲14 **Countable and uncountable nouns**

➲43 **Food and drink (2)**

➲44 **Meals**

People eat …

vegetables meat pasta fish rice eggs fruit bread butter cheese

People drink …

tea coffee milk fruit juice lemonade water

1 Look at this woman's answers. Write sentences with **eats** and **drinks**.

a She eats bread every day.

b She never drinks coffee.

c _____

d _____

e _____

f _____

g _____

Link

every day ➲5B

never ➲9B

verb + -s ➲63

Questionnaire

What do you eat and drink *every day*? Write ✓.
What do you *never* eat or drink? Write ✗.

✓ bread	✓ fruit	☐ rice
☐ cheese	☐ fruit juice	☐ tea
✗ coffee	✗ meat	✓ vegetables
☐ eggs	✗ milk	✓ water
☐ fish	☐ pasta	

2 Look at the examples. Write about you.

_____
_____
_____
_____

I eat rice every day.
I never eat pasta.
I drink milk every day.
I never drink coffee.

B Vocabulary — Fruit and vegetables

FRUIT

MELON ORANGES PINEAPPLE
APPLES BANANAS GRAPES
PEACHES LEMONS STRAWBERRIES

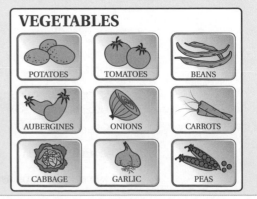

VEGETABLES

POTATOES TOMATOES BEANS
AUBERGINES ONIONS CARROTS
CABBAGE GARLIC PEAS

3 Write answers 1–8 in the diagram.

9 ▼ **10** ▼

1 Orange fruit! ▶

2 A purple vegetable. ▶

3 Small, round, green vegetables. ▶ P E A S

4 They're round and red. ▶

5 Long, yellow fruit. ▶

6 Long, thin, green vegetables. ▶

7 A large, yellow fruit. ▶

8 Small red fruit. ▶

Now complete the sentences:

9▼ Lemons, apples and pineapples are _____ .

10▼ Onions, carrots and potatoes are _____ .

4 Write about you.

I often buy _____ and _____

I don't often buy _____ or _____

I never buy _____ or _____

Links

large, small, thin,
round   ⟳26B

orange, purple,
green   ⟳47A

Links

often, not often ⟳9A

buy   ⟳34A

C Phrases

a kilo of apples

2 kg potatoes	=	two kilos of **potatoes**	2 l water	=	two litres of **water**
1 kg potatoes	=	a kilo of **potatoes**	1 l water	=	a litre of **water**
½ kg potatoes	=	half a kilo of **potatoes**	½ l water	=	half a litre of **water**

5 How much is this man buying?

```
Apples    2.50
Milk      2.40
Cheese    1.25
Water      .70
Onions    1.30
Fish      6.20
--------------
TOTAL    14.35

   Thank you!
```

**Apples
1 kg
2.50**

WATER
1 LITRE
BOTTLE
ONLY -.35!

Onions
1 kg   1.30

**MILK
1 l
-.80**

FISH
Special Offer
1 kg   12.40

Cheese
1 kg
2.50

He's buying (a) *a kilo of apples* , (b) _____ ,

(c) _____ , (d) _____ , (e) _____

and (f) _____ .

Write in your language

I never eat fish.	
I eat fruit every day.	
A kilo of onions, please.	

43 Food and drink (2)

soup, chicken, rice ...; (Chinese) food, a (Chinese) restaurant; sweets, cake, chocolate ...

Food in restaurants

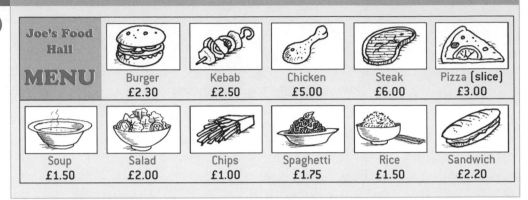

| Joe's Food Hall **MENU** | Burger £2.30 | Kebab £2.50 | Chicken £5.00 | Steak £6.00 | Pizza (slice) £3.00 |
| | Soup £1.50 | Salad £2.00 | Chips £1.00 | Spaghetti £1.75 | Rice £1.50 | Sandwich £2.20 |

1 Match the conversations with the pictures. Complete the conversations.

Links

I'd like, I'll have ➲77C
a bowl of ➲14B

a ☐4 'I'll have _chicken_ with _spaghetti_ , please.'
'OK. That's £6.75.'

b ☐ 'I'd like a ——————— and a bowl of ———————, please.'
'That's £3.70.'

c ☐ 'I'd like two ——————— with ———————, please.'
'OK. That's £6.50, please.'

d ☐ 'I'll have a ——————— and two slices of ———————, please.'
'That's £8.30.'

e ☐ 'I'd like ———————, ——————— and ———————, please.'
'That's £9.00 then, please.'

1

2

3

4

5

An Indian restaurant, Indian food

TAJ MAHAL
RESTAURANT

This is an Indian restaurant.
It has Indian food.
You can eat Indian food here.

2 Complete the sentences. Use words from the box.

Chinese	food	Italian
restaurant	French	
Spanish	American	

ANTONELLI'S
pizza • spaghetti

Le Petit Paris
Bistro

The NEW YORK
burgers • chicken

a You can eat <u>American food</u> at Kentucky Joe's.

b Le Petit Paris has _____ .

c The New York is an _____ .

d You can eat _____ at the New Peking.

e The Flamenco has _____ .

f The Hong Kong is a _____ .

g Antonelli's is a good place for _____ .

KENTUCKY JOE'S
Steak House

NEW PEKING
Restaurant
新北京

FLAMENCO
SPANISH RESTAURANT

香港
H K
O O
N N
G G

Links

Chinese, American … ➔39A

You can … ➔76A

C Vocabulary   Snacks

crisps + ice cream + chocolate + sweets + cake + biscuits =

3 Complete the table (write ✓ or —). What snacks can these people eat?

a John doesn't eat sugar.
<u>He can eat crisps.</u>

b Mary doesn't eat fat.
<u>She</u>

c Tanya doesn't eat flour.

	These have sugar in them.	These have fat in them.	These have flour in them.
crisps	—	✓	—
biscuits	✓	✓	✓
sweets	✓	—	—
ice cream			
cake			
chocolate			

Links

doesn't … ➔65A

can ➔75A

4 Write about you.

I often eat _____

I sometimes eat _____

I never eat _____

Link

often, never, sometimes ➔9B

Write in your language

I'd like chicken, rice and salad, please.

It's a good place for Chinese food.

I don't eat chocolate.

44 Meals

have breakfast/lunch/dinner; have (eggs) for (lunch); knife, fork, spoon, cup ...

A Phrases — breakfast, lunch, dinner

Links

in the morning,
evening ➡5C
You can ... ➡76A
have ➡57A

At the Plaza Hotel, you can ...

... have breakfast from 7.00 to 9.00
in the morning.

... have lunch from 12.00 to 2.00.

... have dinner from 7.30 to 9.30
in the evening.

	breakfast
have	lunch
	dinner

~ PLAZA HOTEL ~

Meals

Breakfast	7.00–9.00
Lunch	12.00–2.00
Dinner	7.30–9.30

1 Complete the sentences. Use **have breakfast**, **have lunch** or **have dinner**.

a I usually _have breakfast_ at 7.00 in the morning.

b On Sunday evening, I always _____ with my parents.

c I finish work at 1.00, then I _____ in a café.

d We _____ at about 9.00 in the evening.

e I always _____ at work at about 12.30.

f You can _____ at the Costa Café from 6.00 in the morning.

B Phrases — We're having eggs for breakfast

Link

➡42, 43 **Food and
drink (1) & (2)**

He's having
eggs for
breakfast.

They're having
sandwiches
for lunch.

We're having
chicken
for dinner.

	breakfast
have ... for	lunch
	dinner

Links

He's having ...
➡57C, 71B
is, are ...-ing
➡69A, B

2 Write about these people.

a He's _having fish and rice for lunch._

b She's _____

c They're _____

d She's _____

e They're _____

f She's _____

a LUNCH TODAY
FISH AND RICE

b 7.00–
9.30 a.m.
☑ eggs
☐ bread
☐ tea
☑ coffee

c Today's special
12.30–2.00
Chicken and Chips

d EVERY
MONDAY EVENING
from 7.30
🍕 PIZZA 🍕

e Dinner Menu
Spaghetti Bolognese

f SNACKS served 12.00-2.00
☑ soup   ☐ cheese sandwich
☐ salad   ☐ burger + chips

Link

bowl, glass, cup ➲14B

a knife   a fork
a glass
a plate
a bowl
a spoon   a cup

Phrases

knife and fork
cup and saucer
salt and pepper

chopsticks   a saucer
pepper
salt

3 What are these things? Write one word in each gap.

a

b

c

a _cup_ and _saucer_   a _____ and _____   _____ and _____

d

e

f

a _____ and a _____   a _____ and a _____   a _____ and _____

4 What are these people eating or drinking? Use words from the box.

Link

has   ➲56A

a ⌷6⌷ Tanya has a cup and saucer.
b ☐ John has a bowl and a spoon.
c ☐ Mona has a small plate and a knife.
d ☐ Tom has a glass.
e ☐ Helen has a large plate, and a knife and fork.
f ☐ Alex has a bowl and chopsticks.

1 chicken and chips
2 mineral water
3 rice
4 soup
5 bread and cheese
✓6 tea

Write in your language

We usually have lunch at 12 o'clock.	
I always have eggs for breakfast.	
Can I have the salt and pepper, please?	

99

45 Adjectives (1)

big, small, hot, cold, cheap, expensive ...; very/quite (big)

A Vocabulary — *a big house*

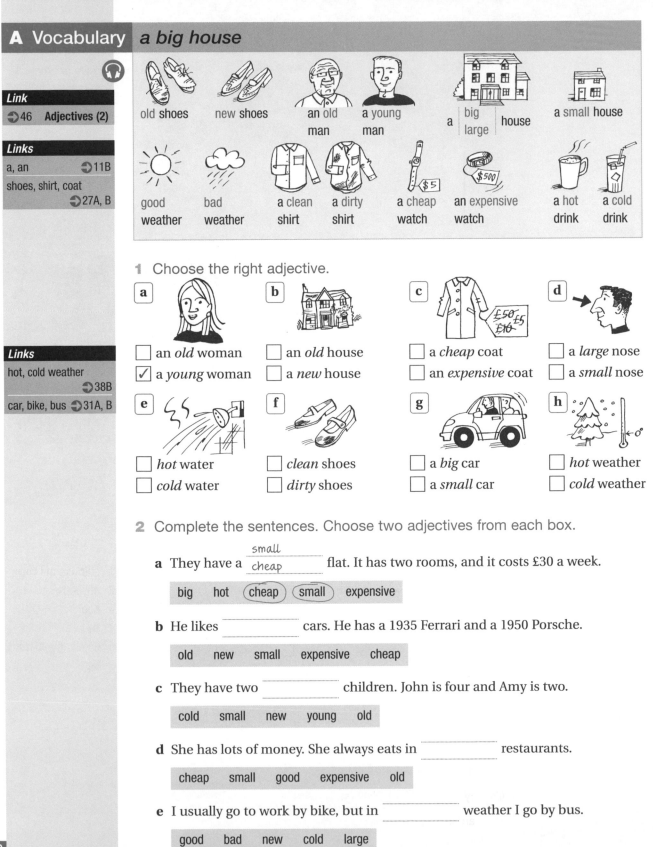

Link
→46 Adjectives (2)

Links
a, an →11B
shoes, shirt, coat →27A, B

old **shoes**   new **shoes**   an old **man**   a young **man**   a big/large **house**   a small **house**

good **weather**   bad **weather**   a clean **shirt**   a dirty **shirt**   a cheap **watch**   an expensive **watch**   a hot **drink**   a cold **drink**

Links
hot, cold weather →38B
car, bike, bus →31A, B

1 Choose the right adjective.

a
☐ an *old* woman
☑ a *young* woman

b
☐ an *old* house
☐ a *new* house

c
☐ a *cheap* coat
☐ an *expensive* coat

d
☐ a *large* nose
☐ a *small* nose

e
☐ *hot* water
☐ *cold* water

f
☐ *clean* shoes
☐ *dirty* shoes

g
☐ a *big* car
☐ a *small* car

h
☐ *hot* weather
☐ *cold* weather

2 Complete the sentences. Choose two adjectives from each box.

a They have a _small / cheap_ flat. It has two rooms, and it costs £30 a week.

    big   hot   (cheap)   (small)   expensive

b He likes _____ cars. He has a 1935 Ferrari and a 1950 Porsche.

    old   new   small   expensive   cheap

c They have two _____ children. John is four and Amy is two.

    cold   small   new   young   old

d She has lots of money. She always eats in _____ restaurants.

    cheap   small   good   expensive   old

e I usually go to work by bike, but in _____ weather I go by bus.

    good   bad   new   cold   large

Link
very, quite →46A

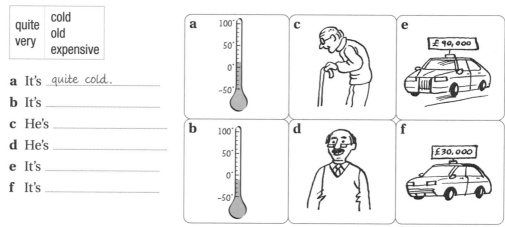

It's very small.   It's quite small.   It's quite big.   It's very big.

3 Complete the sentences. Use words from the table.

quite very	cold old expensive

a It's _quite cold._
b It's ⎯⎯⎯⎯
c He's ⎯⎯⎯⎯
d He's ⎯⎯⎯⎯
e It's ⎯⎯⎯⎯
f It's ⎯⎯⎯⎯

4 Fill the gaps with words from the box.

HOUSE
for rent
£450 a
month

bedroom
bathroom
kitchen
living room

Link
living room,
bedroom ... →41A

The house is (a) _quite small_ – it has a living room, a bedroom, a kitchen and a bathroom. The bathroom is (b) ⎯⎯⎯⎯ , but the living room is (c) ⎯⎯⎯⎯ . And the garden is (d) ⎯⎯⎯⎯ – it's about 200m^2! It's a beautiful house. It's (e) ⎯⎯⎯⎯ – nearly 200 years, in fact. And it's only £450 a month, so it's (f) ⎯⎯⎯⎯ .

quite cheap
quite big
very big
very old
✓quite small
very small

Write in your language

They have an expensive car.	
It's very cold.	
The garden is quite small.	

46 Adjectives (2)

good, bad, wonderful, awful ...; nice, lovely; beautiful/ugly, interesting/boring ...

A Vocabulary *good, bad, wonderful ...*

Link
➡ 45 Adjectives (1)

Link
very, quite ➡ 45B

> We're having a wonderful holiday. The weather's great, the hotel is really good, and the food is excellent.

> We're having an awful holiday. The hotel is terrible, the food is really bad, and the weather's not very good.

← GOOD				BAD →	
wonderful great excellent	very good really good	quite good	not very good	very bad really bad	awful terrible
☺☺☺	☺☺	☺	☹	☹☹	☹☹☹

Link
is, are ➡ 58B

1 Read the reviews. Complete the sentences.

a *In The Dark* is a very good film.

b The story _____

c The actors _____

d John Park's books _____

e *Payback* _____

f The food in Le Bistro _____

g The music _____

h The coffee _____

i *Paper Tiger* _____

j Susie Khan _____

k The songs _____

> **🎬 In The Dark**
> This is a ☺☺ film. The story is ☺, and the actors are ☺☺☺.

> **📖 Payback** *by John Park*
> John Park's books are usually ☺☺, but his new book, *Payback*, is ☹☹☹.

> **☕ Le Bistro,** *Main Road*
> The food is ☹☹, but the music is ☺☺, and the coffee is ☺☺☺.

> **💿 Paper Tiger** *by Susie Khan*
> This CD is ☹. Susie Khan is ☺, but the songs are ☹☹☹.

B Vocabulary *nice, lovely*

> That's a nice **dress**.

> Yes, it's lovely.

☺	➡	☺
nice	very nice	lovely

2 Complete the sentences. Use phrases from the box.

a I like John. He's _a very nice person._ .

b Have _____ at the party.

c That's _____ . Are they your children?

d Get up! It's _____ !

e They have _____ on the coast.

f I like Henri and Jeanne. They're _____ .

very nice people
✓a very nice person
a lovely photo
a lovely house
a nice time
a lovely day

C Vocabulary *beautiful, ugly ...*

a beautiful building   an ugly building   an interesting book   a boring book

a comfortable chair   an uncomfortable chair   a friendly waiter   an unfriendly waiter

= good/nice	= not good/nice
beautiful	ugly
interesting	boring
comfortable	uncomfortable
friendly	unfriendly

---

3 Complete the responses. Choose words from the table.

Link

this, that, these ➲13B

a These flowers are very nice.
Yes, they're _beautiful_ .

b The beds in the hotel are terrible.
Yes, they're very _____ .

c The shop assistants here are awful.
Yes, they're very _____ .

d That film is really good.
Yes, it's very _____ .

e She's very nice. She always says 'Hello'.
Yes, she's very _____ .

f This TV programme is really bad.
Yes, it's very _____ .

Write in your language

It's an excellent restaurant.	
This food is wonderful.	
Have a nice time.	

red, blue, yellow …; is/are (red); a (red) coat; What colour is/are …?

A Vocabulary — *red, blue, yellow …*

Link

➡ 45, 46 **Adjectives (1), (2)**

Links

is, are ➡ 58B

tomatoes, bananas … ➡ 42B

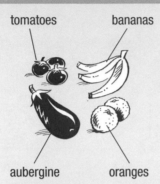

tomatoes   bananas

aubergine   oranges

trees   sky

elephant   wood

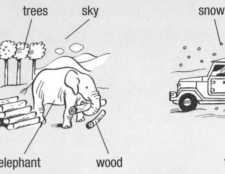

snow

tyre

Tomatoes are red, bananas are yellow, oranges are orange, aubergines are purple.

The sky is blue, trees are green, wood is brown, elephants are grey.

Tyres are black, snow is white.

1 Write the colours.

a The sign is _red_ and _white_ .

b Pandas are _____ and _____ .

c Traffic lights are _____ , _____ and _____ .

d Eggs are _____ and _____ .

e Wasps are _____ and _____ .

f The American flag is _____ , _____ and _____ .

2 Write the missing words in the crossword.

1 blue + red = _ _ _ _ _ _

2 You can go – the lights are _ _ _ _ _ _ .

3 Stop! The lights are _ _ _ !

4 The British flag is red, white and _ _ _ _ .

5 red + green = _ _ _ _ _

6 red + yellow = _ _ _ _ _ _ _

7 He's an old man. He has _ _ _ _ hair.

8 _ _ _ _ _ _ + white = grey

9 blue + _ _ _ _ _ _ = green

10 It isn't a colour TV – it's an old black and _ _ _ _ _ _ TV.

11 The Italian flag is green, _ _ _ and white.

Crossword grid entries:

3 ▶ R E D

B Grammar — *red roses, a blue door*

is/are + colour	colour + noun
Roses are red.	I love red roses.
Our living room is blue.	We have a blue living room.
My eyes are green.	I have green eyes.

3 Put the words in the correct order to make sentences.

a red British are passports   *British passports are red.*

b an dress wearing orange she's   *She's*

c cat a they white have black and

d yellow flag Brazilian the is green and

e her blue hair and are brown is her eyes

f car a she green drives

g roses white six please I'd like

C Phrases — *What colour ...?*

Link

What ...? ➲ 79B

What colour is her coat?

It's grey.

What colour	is ...?
	are ...?

What colour are your eyes?

They're green.

4 Write questions. Use words from the box.

a *What colour are pandas?* — They're black and white.

b _____ — It's red.

c _____ — It's black and white.

d _____ — They're red.

e _____ — It's red and white.

f _____ — They're blue.

British passports
the Japanese flag
their new car
✓ pandas
her eyes
their cat

Write in your language

Are your eyes green or blue?	
I'd like some yellow roses, please.	
What colour are Italian passports?	

105

Hello, how are you?

Hello, Goodbye …; Excuse me, Sorry …; How are you?; I'm / I feel …; hungry, ill, hot …

A Phrases — Hello, goodbye

Link

morning, afternoon …
➜ 5 C

'Hello' words		
Hello	Good morning	Good evening
Hi	Good afternoon	

'Goodbye' words	
Goodbye	Good night
Bye	

1 Choose the right words.

a You see a friend in the street.   (Hi) / ~~Goodbye~~ / ~~Goodnight~~

b It's 8.00. You arrive at work.   Good morning / Good afternoon / Bye

c It's 11.00. You're going to bed.   Goodbye / Good evening / Good night

d It's 5.00. You're leaving work.   Good night / Good morning / Bye

e It's 9.00. You arrive at a restaurant.   Good evening / Good night / Goodbye

f It's 4.00. You see your brother.   Good evening / Hello / Good morning

B Phrases — Excuse me, Sorry …

Link

What's the time?
It's 2 o'clock. ➜ 3A, D

2 Complete the conversations. Write **Excuse me**, **Thank you**, **Sorry** or **That's all right**.

a ' _Excuse me_ . Where's the station?'
'Go down this road and turn right.'
'_____.'

b '_____. Are you Lisa?'
'No, I'm Mary.'
'Oh, _____.'

c '_____. Is this your phone?'
'Yes, it is! _____.'
'_____.'

d '_____. I think that's my pen.'
'Oh, is it? _____. Here you are.'
'_____.'

C Phrases — *How are you?*

Hi. How are you?
I'm OK, thanks.

How is your mother?
Oh, she's not bad.

How are the children?
Oh, they're fine, thanks.

How	are you?		
	is your mother?		
	are the children?		

I'm	fine.	☺
She's	OK.	
They're	not bad.	☺

3 Complete the questions and answers.

a _How is_ your sister?
_____, thanks. ☺

b _____ you?
_____, thanks. ☺

c _____ your parents?
_____ . ☺

d _____ John?
_____ . ☺

D Phrases — *I'm hungry*

I'm hungry. I'm thirsty. I feel tired. I feel ill. I'm hot. I feel cold.

I'm	hungry.
I feel	tired.
	…

4 Match the sentences with the responses.

a I'm tired.
b I'm thirsty.
c I feel hot.
d I'm hungry.
e I'm cold.
f I feel ill.

1 Close the window.
2 Don't go to work today.
3 Have a sandwich.
4 Have a glass of water.
5 Sit down.
6 Take your coat off.

Write in your language

'Hi. How are you?' 'I'm fine, thanks.'	
Excuse me. Is this your phone?	
I'm tired and I'm hungry.	

49 stand, sit, lie ...

stand, sit, lie; stand up, sit down, lie down; walk, run, jump, swim, ride, climb

A Vocabulary

Links

is ...-ing	➲69A
in, on, under, by	➲20
gate, tree, grass ...	➲36
chair, bed, floor, wall ...	➲41

stand, sit, lie

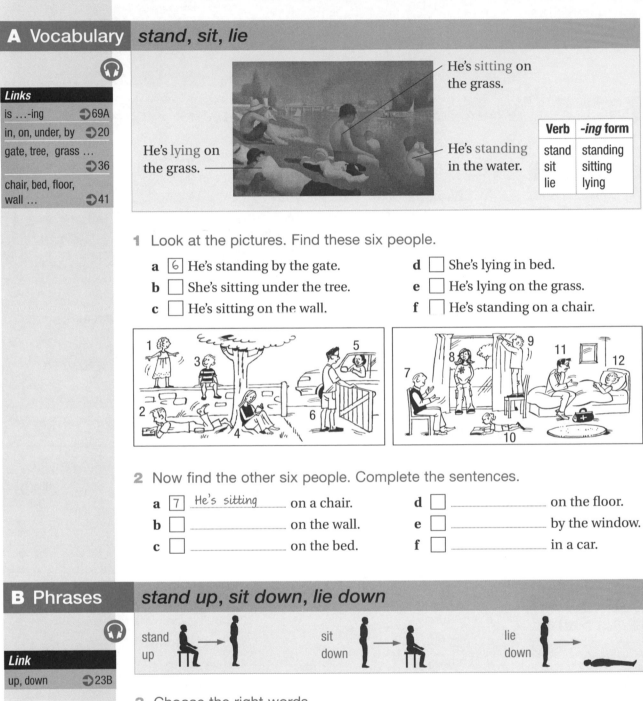

He's sitting on the grass.

He's lying on the grass.

He's standing in the water.

Verb	*-ing* form
stand	standing
sit	sitting
lie	lying

1 Look at the pictures. Find these six people.

a [6] He's standing by the gate.
b ☐ She's sitting under the tree.
c ☐ He's sitting on the wall.
d ☐ She's lying in bed.
e ☐ He's lying on the grass.
f ☐ He's standing on a chair.

2 Now find the other six people. Complete the sentences.

a [7] He's sitting .... on a chair.
b ☐ .... on the wall.
c ☐ .... on the bed.
d ☐ .... on the floor.
e ☐ .... by the window.
f ☐ .... in a car.

B Phrases

Link

| up, down | ➲23B |

stand up, sit down, lie down

stand up

sit down

lie down

3 Choose the right words.

a Take off your shirt and (lie down) / ~~stand up~~ on the bed, please.
b Good morning. Please come in and sit down / stand up .
c I'm tired. I think I'll stand up / lie down for half an hour.
d Sit down / Stand up , everyone. The President is here.
e Let's sit down / lie down and eat our sandwiches.
f Stand up / Lie down – you're sitting on my newspaper.

C Vocabulary   *walk, run, jump ...*

walk   run   jump   swim   climb

4 Complete the sentences.

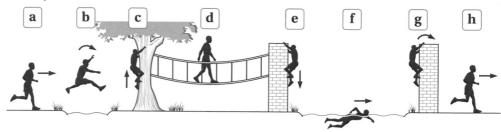

a   b   c   d   e   f   g   h

Links

along, across, up,
down, over   ➲23B

road, stream …
            ➲36A

a You _run_ along a road.
b Then you _____ across a stream.
c Then you _____ up a tree.
d Then you _____ across a bridge.

e Then you _____ down a wall.
f Then you _____ across a river.
g Then you _____ over a wall.
h Then you _____ along a road.

5 Write instructions for this fitness exercise. Use words from the boxes.

Link

➲72   **Imperatives**

Links

on, off   ➲23A
up, down   ➲23B

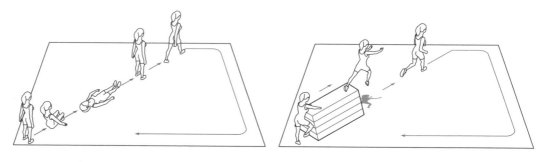

a _Sit down._
b _____
c _____
d _____
e _____
f _____
g _____

walk	up
run	down
stand	on the box
sit	off the box
lie	round the room
climb	
jump	

Write in your language

You're sitting on my chair.	
Please come in and sit down.	
He's lying on the bed.	

50 go and come

go into, come out of; go to, come back from; go to, go for, go ...-ing

A Vocabulary *go, come*

B A N K

They're going
into the bank.

They're coming
out of the bank.

go   come
there   there
here   here

Link
⊃69   **Present
             continuous (2)**

1 Look at the picture. Find the people.

Links
into, out of   ⊃23A
bank, cinema ...
                ⊃35A

a 10 They're coming out of the cinema.   **d** ☐ She's coming out of the hotel.

b ☐ He's going into the café.   **e** ☐ He's going into the bank.

c ☐ She's coming out of the station.

STATION
B A N K
HOTEL
Café
B O O K S   RITZY CINEMA

1 2   3   4   5   6   7   8   9   10

2 Now find the other people. Complete the sentences.

a 5 He's going into the hotel.   **d** ☐ .... the station.

b ☐ .... the cinema.   **e** ☐ .... the bank.

c ☐ .... the bookshop.

B Phrases *go to, come back from*

He's going to Zurich
on 6th February.

He's coming back from
Zurich on 14th February.

Link
⊃71   **Present
             continuous (4)**
Link
6th February   ⊃ 2C

	1	2	3	4	5	6	7	8	9	10	11	12	13	14	15	16
FEB										Zurich						
MAR			Scotland					Frankfurt								
APR							Japan									
MAY			Budapest							Brazil						

3 What is the man doing on these dates?

a He's coming back from Frankfurt on 16th March.

b .... on 8th May.

c .... on 9th March.

d .... on 12th May.

e .... on 15th April.

f .... on 3rd March.

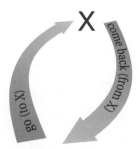

X
come back (from X)
go (to X)

go to the cinema, go for a walk, go shopping

Link

go ...-ing ⮕30B

go to **the cinema**   go for **a walk**   go **shopping**

4 Read about these people. Find expressions with **go** and write them in the table.

What do you do at the weekend?

Lena, 28: We often go to the theatre. Sometimes we go to a concert.

Robin, 26: We have a new car, so we often go for a drive on Sunday.

Paul, 23: On Saturday evening, I usually go for a drink with friends. Or sometimes I go for a meal in a restaurant.

Marie, 32: In the winter, we go skiing in the mountains.

Jean, 14: I sometimes go to the park and play football. Or I go swimming.

go to + noun (go to the cinema)	**go for** + noun (go for a walk)	**go** + verb + **-ing** (go shopping)
go to the theatre		

5 Complete the sentences. Use phrases from the table.

a I don't ➡ 🎭 _go to the theatre_ much, but I often ➡ 🎥

_____ .

b It's a lovely day. Let's ➡ 🚗 _____ .

c They live in Geneva, so they often ➡ ⛷ _____ in the Alps.

d I'm thirsty. Let's ➡ 🥤 _____ .

e We can't ➡ 🛒 _____ today – all the shops are closed.

f We sometimes ➡ _____ on Wednesday evenings.

Write in your language

He's coming back from Paris on Sunday.	
We're going to a concert at the weekend.	
Let's go for a walk.	

51 bring, take, get ...

bring, take; put, take; bring/buy/give me ...; get

A Vocabulary *bring, take*

Link
➔72   **Imperatives**

Take this into the kitchen ...

... and bring the books in here.

there there

here here

TAKE BRING

Link
go, come   ➔50A

1 Complete the sentences. Use bring, bringing, take or taking.

Verb	*-ing* form
bring	bringing
take	taking

a I'm going into town. I'm _taking_ the car.

b Come to my flat this evening and _____ some CDs with you.

c Are you going to the kitchen? Could you _____ me a glass of water?

d I'll _____ you to the airport in the car.

e My son's ill, so I'm _____ him to the doctor.

f Joanna's coming to my birthday party. She's _____ a cake.

B Vocabulary *put, take*

Links
in, on, out of, off ➔23A
keys, money, credit card   ➔40A

Put the money in your pocket.

Take the money out of your pocket.

Put the keys on the table.

Take the keys off the table.

put	the money	in ...
	the keys	on ...

take	the money	out of ...
	the keys	off ...

2 Choose put or take.

a These clothes are clean. I'll (*put*)/ ~~take~~ them in the cupboard.

b *Put / Take* the books out of the box and *put / take* them on the shelf.

c Please *put / take* your feet off the chair.

d *Put / Take* the milk out of the bag and *put / take* it in the fridge.

e Here's your credit card. *Put / Take* it in your pocket.

bring me, buy me, give me ...

Links

Could you ...? ➔77A

apples, bread,
biscuits ... ➔42, 43

bathroom, study,
kitchen, floor ➔41

Could you give me my glasses? = they're here (on the table)

Could you bring me my medicine? = it isn't here (it's in the bathroom)

Could you buy me some apples? = at the shop

Could you	give bring buy	me	...?

3 Complete the sentences.

a Could you bring me _____ a pen? There's one in the study.

b _____ some bread from the supermarket?

c _____ some biscuits from the kitchen?

d Here's ten euros. _____ some oranges?

e _____ the newspaper, please? It's on the floor.

f _____ some water?

get = buy, bring

Link

Shall we ...?,
Let's.... ➔78C

Let's get some bread.

Wait a minute. I'll get my coat from the bedroom.

= Let's buy some bread.   = I'll go to the bedroom and bring my coat.

4 Which meaning – buy or bring?

a Could you go to the chemist and get some tissues?   get = buy

b Could you go to the kitchen and get some water?   get = _____

c Let's get some flowers.   get = _____

d Shall we get a new car?   get = _____

e I'll wait here. Could you go and get the car?   get = _____

f Shall we get a newspaper at the station?   get = _____

Write in your language

I'll take you to the station.	
Could you buy me a newspaper?	
Shall we get some flowers?	

52

Seeing and hearing

see, hear; look at, watch, listen to; look for

A Vocabulary · *see, hear*

Link

can ⟳75A

My hotel is lovely – I can see the beach from my window and I can hear music from a café across the road.

👁️〰️ **see**	👂〰️ **hear**
I can see **the beach**.	I can hear **music**.

1 Which things can you **see**? Which things can you **hear**? Write ✓ or ✗.

	buildings	a plane	the wind	traffic	music	the sea	mountains
You can see …	✓	✓					
You can hear …	✗	✓					

2 Complete the sentences. Use **I can see** or **I can hear**.

Links

near, above ⟳21B, C

in, by ⟳20

a My hotel is near an airport. <u>I can see</u> the airport buildings, and _____ planes all through the night.

b My hotel is above a disco. _____ music all the time.

c I'm staying in the Himalayas. From my room _____ Mount Everest.

d I'm staying in the centre of Paris. _____ the Eiffel Tower.

e My hotel is by the beach. _____ the sea, and _____ it, too!

B Phrases · *look at, watch, listen to*

Link

watch, listen to ⟳55B

You watch a video or DVD.

You listen to a CD.

You look at photos.

3 Read the sentences.
Complete the table.

👁 **look at …**	👁 **watch …**	👂 **listen to …**
photos	a video	a CD

Shh! I'm listening to the radio.

I want to watch the football match this afternoon.

Look at those people. Do you know them?

Shall we watch TV, or shall we listen to music?

Look at this picture. It's by Van Gogh.

4 Are these sentences correct? Write ✓ or correct them.

a Listen to the CD. ✓

b ~~Listen to~~ Look at this picture.

c He often looks at music in the evenings.

d Let's go and look at the football tonight.

e Do you want to listen to my holiday photos?

f The children are watching a film on TV.

g Look at those flowers. They're beautiful.

C Phrases

look at, look for

🎧

Link

is/are …-ing   ⟳ 69

What time is it?

Where's my watch?

She's looking at her watch.

She's looking for her watch.

5 What are the people doing? Write **looking at** or **looking for**.

a She's _looking for_ a job.

b She's _____ her keys.

c He's _____ the stars.

d He's _____ water.

e They're _____ a painting.

f It's _____ food.

Write in your language

I can see the sea from my window.	
Shall we listen to the radio?	
I'm looking for my keys.	

53

Saying and thinking

say, tell; talk to, talk about; ask, answer (a question); I (don't) think

A Vocabulary *say, tell*

Link
hello, thank you
➔ 48A, B

| Say hello to Maria! | Tell Maria I'm at the office. |

| Please phone Maria and say I'm at the office. | Please phone Maria and tell her I'm at the office. |

say	
Say	hello.
	I'm at the office.

tell		
Tell	Maria her	I'm at the office.

1 Complete the notes. Use **say** or **tell**.

a Please phone my parents and _say_ I'll be home at 10.00.

b If you see Amanda, _____ hello from me.

c Please phone Peter. _____ him we're meeting at 6.00.

d Thank you for a great weekend! Please _____ thank you to your parents, too.

e _____ Sue about the party tomorrow.

f George comes home at 6. _____ him there's a pizza in the fridge.

B Phrases *talk to, talk about*

Links
weather, hot, sunny
➔ 38
is ...-ing ➔ 69A

This man is talking to a friend.
He's talking about the weather.

It'll be hot and sunny tomorrow.

talk	to a friend
	about the weather

2 Complete the sentences. Use **talking to** or **talking about** and words from the box.

clothes   football
music   her children
✓ a shop assistant
her father

a A kilo of sugar, please.

b I like Mozart and Vivaldi.

c I need a black dress, shoes and a hat.

d OK, Dad. I'll see you tomorrow. Bye, Dad.

e It's 8.00. Time for school!

f Real Madrid are playing tomorrow.

a She's _talking to a shop assistant._

b She's _____

c She's _____

d She's _____

e She's _____

f She's _____

ask, answer (a question)

Question — What's a papaya?   It's a fruit. — Answer

Noun	Verb
a question	ask a question
an answer	answer a question

She's asking a question.   He's answering the question.

Link

What? Who?   79A

3 Choose the right words.

a Look at the next *question* / *answer* : 'What's 27 × 6?' Do you know the *question* / *answer* ?

b Excuse me. Can I *ask* / *answer* you *a question* / *an answer* ?

c I often send him emails, but he never *asks* / *answers* .

d Who can *question* / *answer* this *question* / *answer* ?

e I'll *ask* / *answer* you three *questions* / *answers* . Can you tell me the *questions* / *answers* ?

D Phrases

I think, I don't think

Link

How old …? He's (16).
   8

'How old is Bill? Is he 16 now?'
'No, I don't think he's 16.
I think he's 17 or 18.'

16?

17?

18?

He's 17. ⟶ I think he's 17.

He isn't 16. ⟶ I don't think he's 16.

NOT ~~I think he isn't 16.~~

4 Look at these photos. What are they? Use **I think** and **I don't think**.

a I don't think it's a flower.
   I think it's an onion.

b ....

c ....

d ....

Links

flower   36B

pasta, milk, onion
   42A, B

chair   41B

fork   44C

hair   26A

a

a flower? an onion?

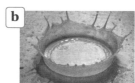
b

milk? a flower?

c

a chair? a fork?

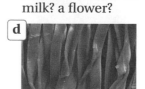
d

hair? pasta?

Write in your language

Tell her about the party.	
Excuse me. Can I ask you a question?	
I don't think he's at the office.	

want, would like, need

want (a sandwich); (don't) want to (go); I'd like (a drink), I'd like to (go); need

A Grammar — *want, want to*

Link

verb (+ -s) ⮐63C

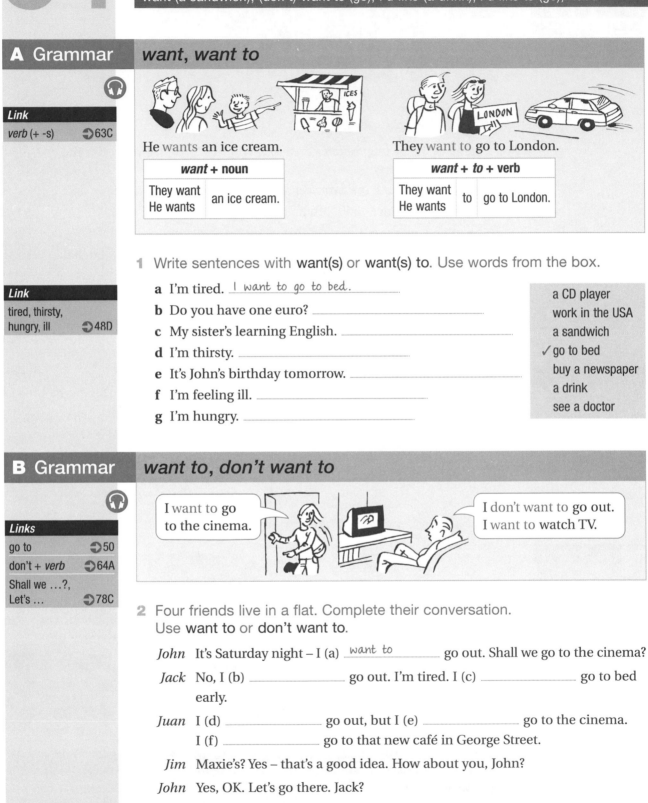

He wants an ice cream.

want + noun	
They want He wants	an ice cream.

They want to go to London.

want + *to* + verb		
They want He wants	to	go to London.

1 Write sentences with **want(s)** or **want(s) to**. Use words from the box.

Link

tired, thirsty,
hungry, ill   ⮐48D

a I'm tired. *I want to go to bed.*

b Do you have one euro? _____

c My sister's learning English. _____

d I'm thirsty. _____

e It's John's birthday tomorrow. _____

f I'm feeling ill. _____

g I'm hungry. _____

> a CD player
> work in the USA
> a sandwich
> ✓ go to bed
> buy a newspaper
> a drink
> see a doctor

B Grammar — *want to, don't want to*

Links

go to   ⮐50

don't + *verb*   ⮐64A

Shall we ...?,
Let's ...   ⮐78C

I want to go to the cinema.

I don't want to go out. I want to watch TV.

2 Four friends live in a flat. Complete their conversation.
Use **want to** or **don't want to**.

John It's Saturday night – I (a) *want to* _____ go out. Shall we go to the cinema?

Jack No, I (b) _____ go out. I'm tired. I (c) _____ go to bed early.

Juan I (d) _____ go out, but I (e) _____ go to the cinema. I (f) _____ go to that new café in George Street.

Jim Maxie's? Yes – that's a good idea. How about you, John?

John Yes, OK. Let's go there. Jack?

Jack No, thanks. I (g) _____ go. Have a nice time!

How many people go to Maxie's café? _____

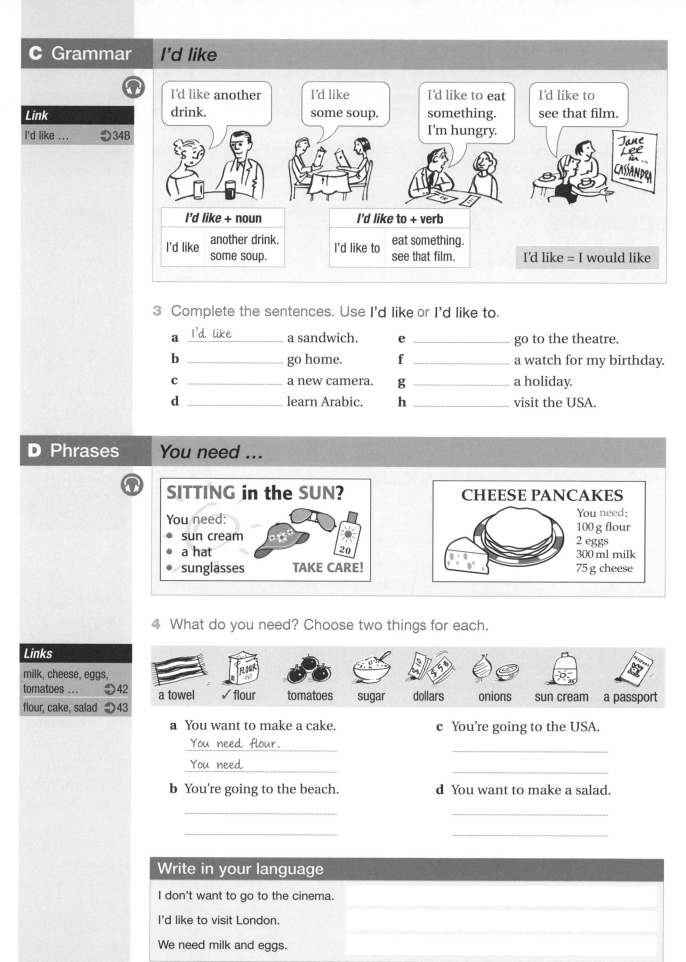

Link

I'd like …   ➲34B

I'd like another drink.

I'd like some soup.

I'd like to eat something. I'm hungry.

I'd like to see that film.

Jane Lee in … CASSANDRA

***I'd like* + noun**	
I'd like	another drink. some soup.

***I'd like* to + verb**	
I'd like to	eat something. see that film.

I'd like = I would like

3 Complete the sentences. Use **I'd like** or **I'd like to**.

a *I'd like* .... a sandwich.

b .... go home.

c .... a new camera.

d .... learn Arabic.

e .... go to the theatre.

f .... a watch for my birthday.

g .... a holiday.

h .... visit the USA.

D Phrases   *You need …*

SITTING in the SUN?

You need:
- sun cream
- a hat
- sunglasses

TAKE CARE!

CHEESE PANCAKES

You need:
100 g flour
2 eggs
300 ml milk
75 g cheese

4 What do you need? Choose two things for each.

Links

milk, cheese, eggs, tomatoes …   ➲42

flour, cake, salad   ➲43

a towel   ✓ flour   tomatoes   sugar   dollars   onions   sun cream   a passport

a You want to make a cake.
You need flour.
You need

b You're going to the beach.

c You're going to the USA.

d You want to make a salad.

Write in your language

I don't want to go to the cinema.	
I'd like to visit London.	
We need milk and eggs.	

55

Everyday activities

wake up, get up, have breakfast, go to work ...; read, write, make ...

A Phrases

get up, have breakfast, go to work

Links

have breakfast, lunch, dinner ➲ 44A, 57A

work, home ➲ 22C

go ➲ 50

Look at this man's day.

He wakes up → gets up → has breakfast → goes to work → starts work ↓

goes to sleep ← goes to bed ← has dinner ← gets home ← finishes work ← has lunch

| wake up
go to sleep | get up
go to bed | have | breakfast
lunch
dinner | | go to work
get home | start
finish | work |

1 Read about Ingrid Braun.

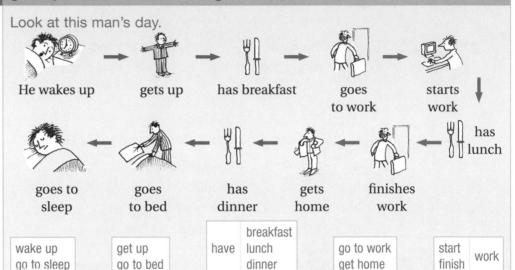

Ingrid gets up at 3.30 in the morning, and works from 4.30 to 11.30.

She has breakfast at work, and she has lunch at home.

She goes to bed at 7.00, and sleeps eight hours every night.

A DAY IN THE LIFE OF ...

INGRID BRAUN
a baker from Frankfurt, Germany

Link

at (3.30) ➲ 4B

Complete the sentences about Ingrid.

a .... at 3.20.
b She gets up .... at 3.30.
c .... at 4.00.
d .... at 4.30.
e She has breakfast .... at 6.00.
f .... at 11.30.

g .... at 12.00.
h She has lunch .... at 1.00.
i .... at 6.00.
j .... at 7.00.
k .... at 7.20.

2 Look at the examples. Write about you and your family.

....
....
....
....

I get up at 7.30.
My brother gets up at 8.00.
I go to work at 8.00, and start work at 9.00.
We have dinner at about 6.30.

B Vocabulary *read, write, make ...*

read	write	watch	listen (to)
She's reading a book.	He's writing a letter.	They're watching TV.	She's listening to the radio.

make	play	wash	clean
He's making coffee.	She's playing the piano.	He's washing the dishes.	He's cleaning his teeth.

3 What are these people doing? Complete the sentences.

a _He's listening to_ music.   **f** _____ cards.

b _____ a video.   **g** _____ a magazine.

c _____ her hair.   **h** _____ an email.

d _____ a cake.   **i** _____ a window.

e _____ a postcard.   **j** _____ the guitar.

4 Write the missing verbs.

a I can't _play_ tennis.

b They often _____ sport on TV.

c I can _____ cakes, but I can't _____ bread.

d I usually _____ a newspaper on the train in the morning.

e I work in a hotel. I _____ the rooms.

f He's only three years old, but he can _____ his name.

Write in your language

I get up at 6.30 and go to work at 7.00.	
She gets home at 6.00 in the evening.	
He's washing his hair.	

56 have (1)

A Grammar — *have, has*

Links

have, has	➲63C
husband, children …	➲28A
phone, mobile	➲40A

We have five phones. We have a phone at home, I have a mobile, my husband has a mobile, and my two children have mobiles.

I We They	have …

He She	has …

1 What other things does the woman say? Add **have** or **has**.

a My husband *has* a motorbike.

b We a computer.

c My son a dog.

d My daughter a bike.

e I an old car.

f We a flat in London.

2 Write about you and your family. Use **have** or **has** and words from the boxes.

I ....

My ....

....

....

I	a car
parents	a bike
mother	a computer
father	a flat in …
brother	a mobile
sister	a …
daughter	

B Grammar — *don't have, doesn't have*

Links

room, shower, bath	➲41
don't	➲64
doesn't	➲65

Hotel Splendide has 100 rooms. All the rooms have showers and baths. The hotel has a swimming pool.

Hotel Capri has 20 rooms. The rooms have showers, but they don't have baths. The hotel doesn't have a swimming pool.

KEY

🛏 60	Rooms
🚿 60	Rooms with shower
🛁 60	Rooms with bath
🍽	Restaurant
🍸	Bar
P	Car park
♒	Swimming pool
🌳	Garden
📺	TV in all rooms

The hotel	has / doesn't have	a swimming pool.

The rooms	have / don't have	baths.

3 Complete the sentences. Use **have**, **don't have**, **has** or **doesn't have**.

    a The Hotel Splendide _has_ a car park.

    b The rooms in the Hotel Splendide _____ a TV.

    c The rooms in the Hotel Capri _____ a TV.

    d The Hotel Capri _____ a restaurant.

    e The Hotel Capri _____ a garden.

    f The Hotel Splendide _____ a garden.

C Phrases

Do you have …?

Links

Do you …?	⟳66A
any	⟳15C
key, pen, money, watch …	⟳40

> Do you have a pen?

> Yes. Here you are.

> Do you have any money?

> No, I don't. Sorry.

Do you have	a pen?
	any money?

4 Add a question. Use **Do you have …?** and words from the box.

… any water?	… a pen?	… a key?	✓… any food?
… a mobile?	… any money?	… a watch?	… a computer?

Link

I'd like, I want, I need …	⟳54

    a I'm hungry. _Do you have any food?_

    b What time is it? _____

    c I'd like to write a letter. _____

    d I want to buy a newspaper. _____

    e I want to send an email. _____

    f I'd like a drink. _____

    g I'd like to phone my mother. _____

    h I want to open the door. _____

Write in your language

She has a flat in Barcelona.	
The hotel doesn't have a car park.	
Do you have a mobile?	

have (2)

have/has lunch, a shower, a party, a good time ...; is/are having (lunch)

A Phrases

have a meal, *have an ice cream*

have a meal

have an ice cream

have a cup of coffee

	have + meals
have has	a meal breakfast lunch dinner

	have + food/drink
have has	a sandwich a pizza a burger an ice cream a cup of coffee

1 Complete the sentences. Use words from the tables.

a I usually *have a cup of coffee* at Castro's.

b We often go to La Bodega to
_____ .

c Maria often _____ at Miller's.

d We sometimes go to Café Dolce and
_____ .

e He never _____ at home.
He always goes to Jo's café.

f I often meet my friends at Mamma's
and we _____ .

MAMMA'S PIZZAS
PIZZA NAPOLI ...
PIZZA ROMANA ...

JO'S
BREAKFAST
ONLY 5.20

MILLER'S
Best burgers
in town!

La Bodega
Business Lunch
12.00–2.00

CASTRO'S
COFFEE HOUSE

CAFÉ
DOLCE for ice cream

B Phrases

have a party, *have a shower*

| It's her birthday. She wants to have a party. | I get up at 7.00 and have a shower. | It's hot. Let's go and have a swim. | We have a meeting every Friday. | I think I'll have a bath and go to bed. |

2 Choose the right word, and add **have** or **has** + **a**.

a We *have a meeting* in New York every month. [*shower / meeting*]

b Why don't you _____ and put on some clean clothes?
[*meeting / bath*]

c 'Is Mr Brown in the office this morning?'
'Yes, he is. But he _____ at 11.00.' [*meeting / bath*]

d My sister always _____ on her birthday. [*meeting / party*]

e I don't want to _____ . The water's cold. [*swim / party*]

f My hair is dirty. I think I'll _____ . [*party / shower*]

C Phrases — *She's having a pizza*

Link
is/are …-ing
⤷69A, B

She's having a pizza.

They're having a meeting.

3 What are these people doing?
Use phrases from A and B.

a He's having a cup of coffee.

b ....

c ....

d ....

e ....

f ....

D Phrases — *Have a good time*

Link
good, nice   ⤷46

Goodbye! Have a nice time.

Have a good holiday.

Links
weekend, day,
morning …   ⤷5
go to, go …-ing
⤷50C, 30B

4 What can you say to these people? Write sentences from the table.

a Some friends are going to London for the weekend.

  Have a nice time.   Have a good weekend.

b It's 7.30 in the morning. Your husband/wife is going to work.

  ....

c Some friends are going skiing for two weeks in France.

  ....

d A friend is going to a restaurant for dinner.

  ....

e It's 5.00 on Friday afternoon. You're saying goodbye to a friend at work.

  ....

		time.
		day.
Have a	good	evening.
	nice	weekend.
		meal.
		holiday.

Write in your language

I usually have a sandwich for lunch.	
They're having a meeting on Friday.	
Have a good weekend.	

58 be (1)

I'm, you're, we're; is, are; he's, she's, it's, they're

A Grammar — *I'm, you're, we're*

Link
I, you, we ➲17A

I'm Donna.

Hi. I'm Mike.

I'm Doctor Phillips.

Ah – you're a doctor …

So, you're German …

Yes – we're from Berlin.

I'm   (= I am)
you're   (= you are)
we're   (= we are)

1 Add the missing verbs. Write the sentences.

a Hi. I Julia. I from London.   *Hi. I'm Julia. I'm from London.*

b Happy Birthday! You 16 today!   ....

c Hello. I John. I a student.   ....

d We Japanese. We from Osaka.   ....

e Mr Williams … Yes, you in Room 235.   ....

B Grammar — *is, are*

Links

black, white, grey
➲47A

dress, shoes, hat, coat ➲27A, B

wall, floor, chair
➲41B, C

This painting is mostly grey and black.
The woman's dress is black, her shoes are black, and her chair is black.
The wall and the floor are grey.

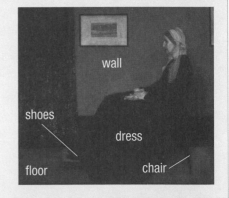

wall

shoes

dress

floor

chair

Singular	**Plural**
Her dress is black. The wall is grey.	Her shoes are black. The wall and the floor are grey.

2 Look at this painting. Write **is** or **are**.

The sky (a) *is* grey, the clouds (b) .... white, and the mountains (c) .... black. The road (d) .... grey. The man's hat and coat (e) .... black, and the dog (f) .... black and white.

hat   clouds   mountains

sky

coat

road

dog

C Grammar — *he's, she's, it's, they're*

Links

his, their ➥ 19B

wife, children ➥ 28A

This is King Abdullah II.
He is
He's   the King of Jordan.

This is Queen Rania.
She is
She's   his wife.

This is Prince Hussein …

… this is Princess Iman …

… and this is Princess Salma.

This is their home.
It is
It's   in Amman.

They are
They're their children.

He is …	She is …	It is …	They are …
OR	OR	OR	OR
He's …	She's …	It's …	They're …

❗ This is, NOT ~~This's~~

---

3 Write the sentences with 's or 're.

a They are Chinese. *They're Chinese.*   **d** He is 24. ....

b She is a doctor. ....   **e** It is a nice day. ....

c It is four o'clock. ....   **f** They are married. ....

---

4 Complete the sentences. Use **He's**, **She's**, **It's** or **They're**.
Match the sentences with the pictures.

a ☐5☐ These are my parents.
  They're quite old now.

b ☐ This is my car.
  .... a 1965 Buick.

c ☐ This is my husband, Michel.
  .... French.

d ☐ This is my daughter, Lise.
  .... nearly 15.

e ☐ These are our two dogs.
  .... Dalmatians.

f ☐ This is our flat.
  .... in the centre of Paris.

Verb tables

be

page 172

Write in your language

I'm English, and my wife is German.

They're Japanese.

It's a nice day.

59 be (2)

A Grammar   *I'm not ...*

Link

➲ 58   **be (1)**

I'm cold.   I'm not cold.

I'm ➡ I'm not (= I am not)

Links

cold, hungry, tired, thirsty   ➲ 48D

Italian, French, American   ➲ 39A

1 Complete the sentences. Use **I'm** or **I'm not**.

   a I have an Italian name, but _I'm not_ Italian.

   b Can I have some bread, please? _____ hungry.

   c I don't want to go to bed. _____ tired.

   d I live in Paris, but _____ French. I'm American.

   e Hello. _____ Miguel. What's your name?

   f 'Do you want some water?' 'No, thanks. _____ thirsty.'

B Grammar   *isn't, aren't*

is ➡ isn't (= is not)
are ➡ aren't (= are not)

The café is open.   The shops are open.   The café isn't open.   The shops aren't open.

Links

family, brother, son ...   ➲ 28A

...'s   ➲ 19C

2 The picture shows two families. Read the sentences. Choose **isn't** or **aren't**.

   a Alan and Mary ~~isn't~~ / (aren't) married.

   b John *isn't* / *aren't* Charles's son.

   c Alan *isn't* / *aren't* Susie's father.

   d The two boys *isn't* / *aren't* brothers.

   e The two girls *isn't* / *aren't* sisters.

Alan Mary Flora Charles

Susie Julia Nick John

Who is in Family 1? _Alan,_____

Who is in Family 2? _____

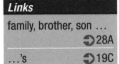

Link

Russian, German
↪ 39A

Maria Sharapova, the American tennis player

She isn't
She's not American – she's Russian.

French cars: BMW and Mercedes

They aren't
They're not French – they're German.

Positive	Negative	
I'm	I'm not	–
you're	you're not	you aren't
we're	we're not	we aren't
they're	they're not OR	they aren't
he's	he's not	he isn't
she's	she's not	she isn't
it's	it's not	it isn't

3 Complete the responses. Use negative sentences.

Link

fax machine,
photocopier ↪ 32D

a I think they're Italian.

They're not Italian. OR *They aren't Italian.*   They're French.

b I'm ten today!

_____ You're only nine.

c … Steven Spielberg, the German film director …

_____ He's American.

d Good evening, Mr and Mrs Jones.

_____ We're Mr and Mrs Brown.

e It's 5 o'clock. Let's go.

_____ It's 4.30.

f I like your new shoes.

_____ They're quite old.

g Can I use this photocopier?

_____ It's a fax machine.

h That's Sophie. I think she's his wife.

_____ She's his sister.

Verb tables

be
page 172

Write in your language

They aren't married.	
She isn't Italian – she's French.	
No, thanks. We're not hungry.	

60 be (3)

Are you …?, Is it …?; Yes, I am, No, it isn't…; Where/What/Who (is) …?

A Grammar — Are you …?

Link
➜ 58, 59 **be (1), (2)**

Links
English, Spanish …
➜ 39A

waiter, doctor, teacher
➜ 29A

> Are you English?
>
> Yes, we are. We're from London.
>
> Are you married?
>
> Yes, I am.
>
> Excuse me. Are you a waiter?
>
> No, I'm not!

| Are you | English? married? a waiter? | Yes, I am. No, I'm not. |

| **Sentence** | → | **Question** |
| You are English. | | Are you English? |

1 Put the words in the correct order to make questions. Answer about you. Use **Yes, I am** or **No, I'm not**.

a you a doctor are ? — Are you a doctor? — ....

b Brazil from are you ? — .... — ....

c Spanish you are ? — .... — ....

d are married you ? — .... — ....

e a are teacher you ? — .... — ....

B Grammar — Is the hotel nice?

Links
nice, lovely, friendly, comfortable ➜ 46B, C

clean, cheap ➜ 45A

> … Is the hotel nice?
>
> Yes, it's lovely.
>
> Are the beds comfortable?
>
> Yes, they're fine.

| **Sentence** |
| The hotel is nice. The beds are comfortable. |
| ↓ |
| **Question** |
| Is the hotel nice? Are the beds comfortable? |

2 Your friend is in San José. Ask questions.

a Is the weather good? ....

b ....

c ....

d ....

e ....

f ....

Come to San José …

★ the weather's good
★ the water's warm
★ the beaches are clean
★ the people are friendly
★ the food is good …
★ … and it's cheap, too.

C Phrases — *Yes, it is, No, it isn't*

Link

isn't, aren't ➲59B

Is the weather good? → Yes, it is. It's lovely.

Is the weather good? → No, it isn't. It's cold and wet.

Are they American? → Yes, they are. They're from New York.

Are they American? → No, they aren't. They're English.

3 Write short answers.

a	Is Paula 18?	*No, she isn't.*	She's only 17.
b	Is their flat nice?		It's lovely.
c	Are the children at home?		They're in bed.
d	Is John at home?		He's at work.
e	Is this your car?		I don't have a car.
f	Is she Spanish?		She's from Madrid.
g	Are you from Washington?		We're from Boston.

Yes,	he is. she is. it is. we are. they are.

No,	he isn't. she isn't. it isn't. we aren't. they aren't.

D Phrases — *Who? What? Where?*

Link

➲79 Question words (1)

For Sale EUPHONIUM — What is a euphonium?

2 WEEKS' HOLIDAY IN SAN JOSÉ — Where is San José?

7.30 MY LIFE: Alice Porter talks about her life — Who is Alice Porter?

LIMA BEANS 1 kilo — What are lima beans?

For Sale HOUSE in the Virgin Islands — Where are the Virgin Islands?

BOB and JO *in concert* TONIGHT — Who are Bob and Jo?

4 Ask questions with What? Where? or Who?

a	You need 2 kilos of (damsons,) 1 kilo of sugar,	*What are damsons?*
b	He has a house in (the Black Mountains)	
c	(The Sax People) are playing at Pete's Jazz Bar tonight	
d	(John Dando) will talk about his new book	
e	She lives in the town of (Gbinsk)	
f	You can buy a small (hammer) for only £2	

Verb tables

be page 172

Write in your language

'Is he English?' 'No, he isn't.'	
Are the children at home?	
Where is their flat?	

131

61 There is/are

There's ..., There are ...; There isn't a ..., There aren't any ...

A Grammar

Link
➲58   **be (1)**

Links
bank, hotel,
post office ... ➲35A
beach, river, lake
      ➲37A

There are three hotels

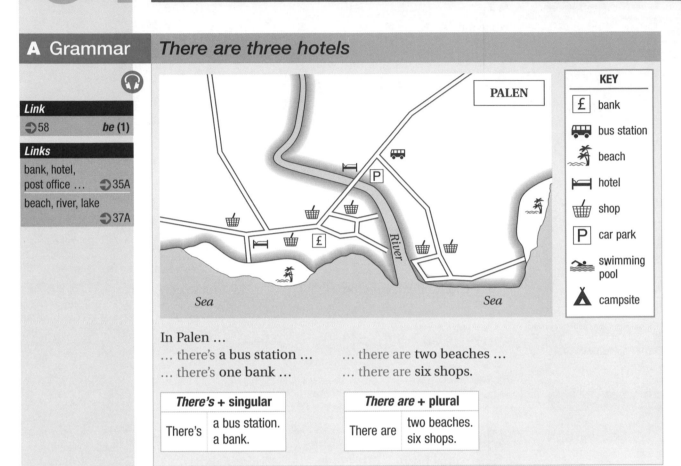

KEY

£	bank
	bus station
	beach
	hotel
	shop
P	car park
	swimming pool
	campsite

In Palen ...

... there's **a bus station** ...   ... there are **two beaches** ...

... there's **one bank** ...   ... there are **six shops**.

There's + singular	
There's	a bus station.
	a bank.

There are + plural	
There are	two beaches.
	six shops.

1 Write sentences about Trandino. Use **There's ...** or **There are ... .**

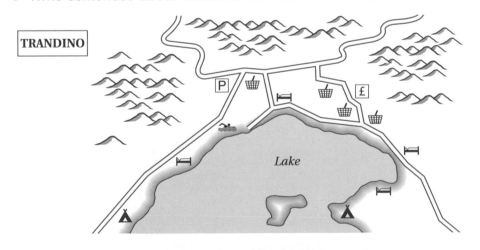

a £   There's a bank.   **d** P ....

b ⊨ ....   **e** ⛺ ....

c ⛶ ....   **f** ≋ ....

B Grammar   *There aren't any hotels*

Link

➲59   *be (2)*

Link

any   ➲15C

On Bird Island ...

... there isn't **a bank** and there isn't **a bus station.** There aren't **any hotels** and there aren't **any car parks.** There's only a lighthouse – and a lot of birds.

Bird Island

lighthouse

There isn't + singular	
There isn't	a bank.
	a bus station.

There aren't + plural	
There aren't	any hotels.
	any car parks.

2 Look at A. Are these sentences about Palen or Trandino? Write **P** or **T**.

a ☐T There isn't a river.   **d** ☐ There isn't a bus station.

b ☐ There aren't any campsites.   **e** ☐ There isn't a lake.

c ☐ There aren't any swimming pools.   **f** ☐ There aren't any beaches.

3 Look at the picture for 30 seconds. Then don't look, and write true sentences.

a women   *There are three women.*

b men   *There aren't any men.*

c dogs   *There's one dog.*

d cats

e children

f hotels

g tables

h bikes

Link

women, men, children

➲10C

Verb tables

There is/are
page 172

Write in your language

There's a bus station in Palen.	
There are three hotels.	
There aren't any shops.	

Is/Are there ...?

Is there a ...?, Are there any ...?; How many ... are there?

A Grammar   *Is there a supermarket near here?*

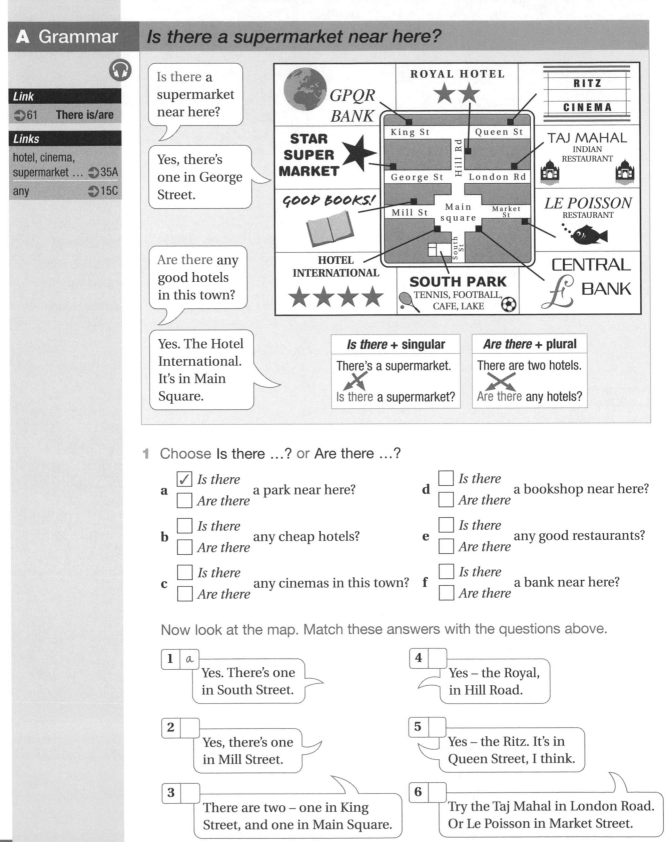

Link

➜61   **There is/are**

Links

hotel, cinema, supermarket ... ➜35A

any   ➜15C

Is there a supermarket near here?

Yes, there's one in George Street.

Are there any good hotels in this town?

Yes. The Hotel International. It's in Main Square.

Is there + singular	*Are there* + plural
There's a supermarket.	There are two hotels.
Is there a supermarket?	Are there any hotels?

1 Choose **Is there ...?** or **Are there ...?**

a ✓ *Is there* / ☐ *Are there*   a park near here?

b ☐ *Is there* / ☐ *Are there*   any cheap hotels?

c ☐ *Is there* / ☐ *Are there*   any cinemas in this town?

d ☐ *Is there* / ☐ *Are there*   a bookshop near here?

e ☐ *Is there* / ☐ *Are there*   any good restaurants?

f ☐ *Is there* / ☐ *Are there*   a bank near here?

Now look at the map. Match these answers with the questions above.

1 | a   Yes. There's one in South Street.

2 | Yes, there's one in Mill Street.

3 | There are two – one in King Street, and one in Main Square.

4 | Yes – the Royal, in Hill Road.

5 | Yes – the Ritz. It's in Queen Street, I think.

6 | Try the Taj Mahal in London Road. Or Le Poisson in Market Street.

2 Complete the questions. Use **Is there ...?** or **Are there ...?**

a ___Are there___ any good shops?

b _____ a café near here?

c _____ a post office near here?

d _____ any good museums?

e _____ any toilets near here?

f _____ a school in this town?

B Phrases

Links

bath, shower	➲41B
have, has	➲56A
How many ...?	➲16C

How many rooms are there?

ROYAL HOTEL ★★★

The Royal Hotel has five single rooms, twelve double rooms and four family rooms.

• The single rooms have one bed and a shower. 🛏 5

• The double rooms have two beds and a bath. 🛏 12

• The family rooms have three beds, a bath and a shower. 🛏 4

The hotel also has a bar 🍸 1 and two restaurants. 🍽 2

How many **double rooms** are there in the Royal Hotel?

Twelve.

How many **restaurants** are there?

Two.

	Sentence		Question	
There are	twelve double rooms. two restaurants.	→	How many	double rooms restaurants	are there?

3 Look at the answers. What are the questions? Use words from the box.

| showers | beds | bars | baths | ✓family rooms | rooms |

a ___How many family rooms are there?___

Four.

b _____

Nine.

c _____

One.

d _____

Twenty-one.

e _____

Sixteen.

f _____

Forty-one.

Verb tables

There is/are
page 172

Write in your language

Is there a good hotel in this town?	
Are there any shops near here?	
How many single rooms are there?	

63 Present simple (1)

I/We/They (live) ...; He/She (lives) ...; have, study, work, go ...

A Grammar — We live in Arizona

Link

have ⟶ 56A

Welcome to my Website!

Hi! I'm Pete Simpson. I'm 35, I'm married, and I (have) three children. We (live) in Tucson, Arizona.

Clarisa's Home page

I'm Clarisa Gonzalez. I'm 19, I (live) in Mendoza in Argentina, and I (study) music at the university.

1 Here are some sentences from the two websites. Find verbs and write them in the table.

	have
	live
I	study
You	play
We	
They	

a I (play) the violin, the piano and the guitar.

b I play baseball with my children every Saturday.

c My parents work in Mendoza. They teach English at a high school.

d I work for a small computer company.

e My children go to high school in the city.

f I have a 12-year-old brother, Oswaldo.

g We all like baseball in our family.

h At home, we speak Spanish, and sometimes English.

2 Read the sentences again. Are they about Pete or Clarisa? Write P or C.

a C   b ____   c ____   d ____   e ____   f ____   g ____   h ____

B Grammar — She lives in London

Links

watch, play ⟶ 30A, 55B

watch, play, read ... ⟶ 55B

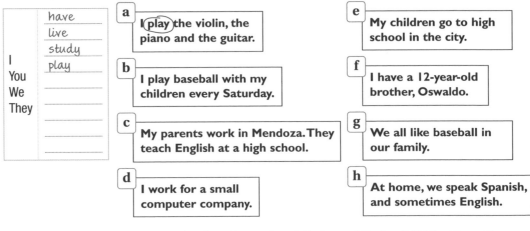

Kate Smith lives in London.

She reads magazines.

She plays tennis.

She watches sport.

She studies French.

She drinks black coffee.

drink play read	He She	drinks plays reads	live watch study	He She	lives watches studies

3 Complete the sentences about Jim Brown.

a He plays ———— chess.
b ———————— tea.
c ———————— films.
d ———————— a newspaper.
e ———————— geography.
f ———————— in Oxford.

C Grammar

work, works ...

Link

-s, -es ...   ➲10B

Verb + *-s*		Verb + *-es*		-*y* → -*ies*		Irregular	
drink	drinks	watch	watches	study	studies	have	has
speak	speaks	teach	teaches				
work	works	go	goes				
read	reads						
like	likes						
live	lives						
play	plays						

4 Fill the gaps with the correct form of the verb.

My brother Rudi is German, but he (a) has ———— (have) a Spanish
wife, called Lucia. Rudi and Lucia (b) ———————— (live) in Montreal, in
Canada, and they (c) ———————— (work) at the university. Lucia
(d) ———————— (teach) geography, and Rudi (e) ———————— (teach)
German. They (f) ———————— (speak) French at work, but at home they
usually (g) ———————— (speak) German. They (h) ———————— (have) a
19-year-old daughter, Heidi, and a 10-year-old son, André. Heidi
(i) ———————— (study) French and German at university. André
(j) ———————— (go) to an English school, and he (k) ———————— (speak)
Spanish, German, French and English.

Links

German, Spanish ...
                ➲39C
at work, at home
                ➲22C

Verb tables

Present simple
page 173

Write in your language

My parents live in London.	
He speaks French and Spanish.	
She teaches geography.	

Present simple (2)

I don't (work); I don't know, I don't understand; We/You/They don't …

A Grammar

Link
→63   **Present simple (1)**

Link
work   →29

Links
eat, drink	→42A
have	→56
speak	→39C
watch, play	→30A, 55B

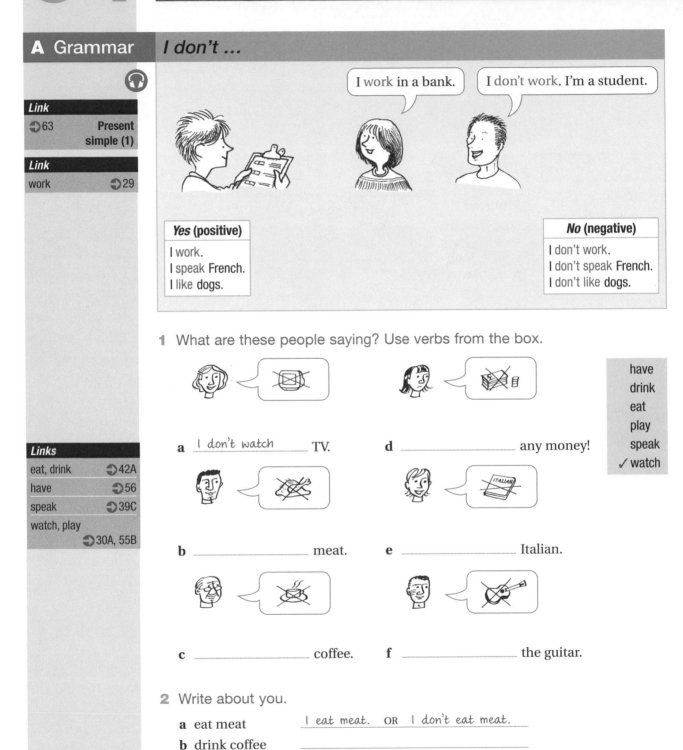

I don't …

I work in a bank.

I don't work. I'm a student.

Yes (positive)	*No* (negative)
I work.	I don't work.
I speak French.	I don't speak French.
I like dogs.	I don't like dogs.

1 What are these people saying? Use verbs from the box.

a I don't watch _____ TV.

d _____ any money!

b _____ meat.

e _____ Italian.

c _____ coffee.

f _____ the guitar.

> have
> drink
> eat
> play
> speak
> ✓ watch

2 Write about you.

a eat meat   I eat meat. OR I don't eat meat.

b drink coffee   _____

c work   _____

d have long hair   _____

e speak Japanese   _____

f have children   _____

B Phrases   *I don't know, I don't understand*

Link

What's …?
Where's …?   ⟳79A

What's 16 × 12?	I don't know.
日本語を話しますか?	Sorry – I don't understand.

3 What are the answers? Write **I don't know** or **I don't understand**.

a Where's the station?   I don't know.

b How old is Peter?

c Ina ga jiya?

d Govorite hrvatski?

e What's her phone number?

f Πώς σε λένε;

C Grammar   *we don't, you don't, they don't*

'Let's take a taxi.'
'We can't. We don't have any money.'

'I want a guitar for my birthday.'
'You don't play the guitar.'
'I know, but I want to learn.'

'Mr and Mrs Brown?'
'Sorry. They don't live here.'

We You They	don't	have … eat … live …

4 Write **don't** + verb. Use verbs from the box.

a They're married, but they *don't have* children.

b They speak French, but they _____ English.

c We have a TV, but we _____ it very often.

d We _____ in London. We live in Oxford.

e I have a brother, but you _____ him.

f They go to work by bus. They _____ a car.

speak
know
✓ have
have
live
watch

Verb tables

Present simple
page 173

Write in your language

I don't smoke.	
Sorry – I don't understand.	
They don't speak Spanish.	

65 Present simple (3)

He/She doesn't (go); likes, doesn't like; He/She doesn't (eat), They don't (eat)

A Grammar — *He doesn't go out*

Link

➲63 **Present simple (1)**

Links

play tennis, football
➲30A

go ➲50C

watch, listen, read …
➲55B

My son John doesn't go out … | He doesn't play football … | He doesn't go to the cinema … | He doesn't listen to pop music …

He doesn't play computer games … | He doesn't even watch TV … | He just sits in his room … | … and reads books.

1 Complete the table.

	Yes (positive): verb + -s		No (negative): doesn't + verb
He She	goes … plays … listens … watches … sits … reads …	He She	*doesn't go* *doesn't play*

2 Write **doesn't** + verb. Use verbs from the box.

a My sister *doesn't work* in Berlin. She works in Hamburg.

b My brother _____ to school. He goes to university.

c He has two cats, but he _____ a dog.

d She _____ jeans to work. She wears a dress.

e He speaks English and French, but he _____ German.

f Richard _____ in New York. He lives in Washington.

g Ivan plays tennis, but he _____ football.

go
have
live
play
speak
wear
✓ work

B Grammar — *She doesn't like …*

She likes dogs. | She doesn't like dogs. | He likes meat. | He doesn't like meat.

3 Write about these people. Use **likes** or **doesn't like**.

a He likes books.

b _____

c _____

d _____

e _____

f _____

a	b	c
books	cats	school

d	e	f
pop music	children	birthdays

C Grammar *doesn't, don't*

He She My father John	doesn't	like fish. eat meat.

They My parents John and Alex	don't	like fish. eat meat.

Links

They don't … ➔64C

cheese, onion, tomato … ➔42

4 Mr and Mrs Brown go to a pizza restaurant with their children and their friends, Alex and Jodie. They don't like the same food.

Choose **don't** or **doesn't**.

a Mr Brown ☐ *don't* ☑ *doesn't* eat onions.

b Mrs Brown ☐ *don't* ☐ *doesn't* like mushrooms.

c The children ☐ *don't* ☐ *doesn't* eat olives.

d Alex and Jodie ☐ *don't* ☐ *doesn't* eat tuna.

e Alex ☐ *don't* ☐ *doesn't* like sausage.

PIZZAS

Venezia — olives, onions, tomatoes

Al pollo — chicken, cheese, tomatoes

Tonno — tuna, cheese, tomatoes

Napolitana — cheese, tomatoes, olives

Americana — sausage, cheese, tomatoes, onions

Al funghi — mushrooms, cheese, tomatoes, onions

They want just one large pizza.

Which pizza can they all eat?

Answer: _____

Verb tables

Present simple
page 173

Write in your language

She doesn't speak English.	
He doesn't have a computer.	
She doesn't like children.	

66 Present simple (4)

Do you ...?; Yes, I do / No, I don't; What / Where / When / How much do you ...?

A Grammar — *Do you wake up early?*

Links

wake up,
go to work ... ➔ 55A

have a shower,
breakfast ... ➔ 57A, B

before, after ➔ 4D

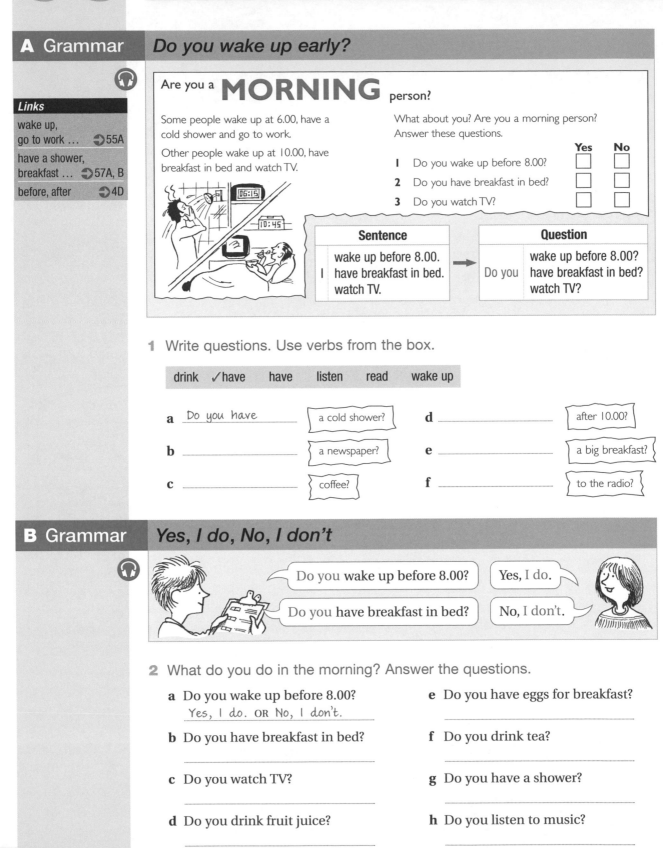

Are you a MORNING person?

Some people wake up at 6.00, have a cold shower and go to work.

Other people wake up at 10.00, have breakfast in bed and watch TV.

What about you? Are you a morning person? Answer these questions.

		Yes	No
1	Do you wake up before 8.00?	☐	☐
2	Do you have breakfast in bed?	☐	☐
3	Do you watch TV?	☐	☐

Sentence		Question
I wake up before 8.00. have breakfast in bed. watch TV.	→ Do you	wake up before 8.00? have breakfast in bed? watch TV?

1 Write questions. Use verbs from the box.

> drink ✓have have listen read wake up

a Do you have _____ { a cold shower? } **d** _____ { after 10.00? }

b _____ { a newspaper? } **e** _____ { a big breakfast? }

c _____ { coffee? } **f** _____ { to the radio? }

B Grammar — *Yes, I do, No, I don't*

Do you **wake up** before 8.00? Yes, I do.

Do you **have** breakfast in bed? No, I don't.

2 What do you do in the morning? Answer the questions.

a Do you wake up before 8.00?
Yes, I do. OR No, I don't.

b Do you have breakfast in bed?

c Do you watch TV?

d Do you drink fruit juice?

e Do you have eggs for breakfast?

f Do you drink tea?

g Do you have a shower?

h Do you listen to music?

Where do you work?

Link

What, When,
Where ...? ➲79

Read the interview.

Kelly	What do you do, Tan Liu?
Tan	I'm a waiter.
Kelly	And where do you work?
Tan	In a Chinese restaurant in Soho.
Kelly	When do you start work?
Tan	At 12.30 in the afternoon.

What		do?
Where	do you	work?
When		start work?

❗ NOT

~~What you do?~~
~~Where you work?~~

TALK TIME

This week Kelly Brown talks to **Tan Liu**, a waiter in a Chinese restaurant in Soho.

3 Read the magazine article. Find the seven verbs.

4 Complete the questions.

a *Kelly* Where <u>do you come from?</u>
   Tan From Hong Kong.

b *Kelly* Where _____
   Tan In London.

c *Kelly* When _____
   Tan At 11.30 in the evening.

d *Kelly* How much _____
   Tan About £400 a week.

e *Kelly* What _____
   Tan English and maths.

f *Kelly* Where _____
   Tan At a college near the restaurant.

TAN LIU (comes) from Hong Kong. He lives in London, and he works in a Chinese restaurant in Soho. He starts work at 12.30 in the afternoon, and he finishes work at 11.30 in the evening. He earns about £400 a week.

In the morning, he studies English and maths at a college near the restaurant.

Verb tables

Present simple
page 173

Write in your language

'Do you have lunch at work?'

'No, I don't.'

Where do you work?

Present simple (5)

Does he/she ...?, Do they ...?; What / Where / When / What time (does) ...?

A Grammar

Does he work in a hospital?

Link

➜ 63, 66   **Present simple (1), (4)**

Links

nurse, teacher, hospital ...   ➜ 29A

brother, sister, parents ...   ➜ 28A

My brother's a nurse.

Does he **work** in a hospital?

No, he doesn't. He works in a school. He's the school nurse.

Jane and Alan are in Tokyo.

Do they **live** there?

Yes, they do. They teach English at a language school.

Question				Answer
Does	he	work in a hospital?	→	Yes, he/she does.
	she	live in Tokyo?		No, he/she doesn't.

Do they	live in Tokyo?	→	Yes, they do.
	work in a hospital?		No, they don't.

1 Complete the questions and answers.

a 'My sister works in a hotel.'

'_Does she_ like it?'

'_No, she doesn't_ . She says it's very boring.'

b 'My parents are teachers.'

'................................ teach children?'

'................................ . They teach at the university.'

c 'I'm going to Bristol to see my brother.'

'................................ live there?'

'................................ . He studies at Bristol University.'

d 'Miranda is a secretary.'

'................................ work in an office?'

'................................ . She works in a bookshop.'

B Grammar

Where do kangaroos live?

Link

What, Where ...?   ➜ 79A

Q Where do kangaroos live?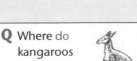

A In Australia.

Q What do penguins eat?

A Fish.

Q What does Lleyton Hewitt play?

A Tennis.

Q Where does sushi come from?

A Japan.

What	does	he she it	...?

What	do they	...?

| Where | | |

| Where | | |

2 Write questions. Match them with the answers in the box.

| 1 India and Africa. | 3 In the White House. | 5 The guitar. |
| 2 Italy. | 4 In Antarctica. | 6 Football. |

a Where / penguins / live?   *Where do penguins live?*   4

b What / Eric Clapton / play?

c Where / elephants / come from?

d Where / Fiat cars / come from?

e What / Ronaldo / play?

f Where / the US President / live?

C Phrases

What time does the bus leave?

Links

When, What time …?   ➲79C

open, close   ➲34C

leave, arrive   ➲31C

at half past, twenty past   ➲4B

| What time does the bus leave? | At about eleven o'clock. | When does the shop close? | At half past five. | What time does the film start? | At 7.45. |

When What time	does	the bus leave? the shop close? the film start?

3 Look at the answers. What are the questions? Use verbs from the box.

| leave | open | start | arrive | ✓close | finish |

a *What time does the library close?*
At half past four.

b
At six o'clock.

c
At half past three.

d
At twenty past five.

e
At nine o'clock in the evening.

f
At half past nine.

Please come to my
♦ PARTY! ♦
6.00 - 9.00
My place

Lewisham
LIBRARY
Open: 9.30 – 4.30
Monday – Saturday

Take the 3.30 train from London
Waterloo. I'll see you at
Manchester station at 5.20.
V

Verb tables

Present simple
page 173

Write in your language

Does she work in a hospital?	
Where does sushi come from?	
What time does the bus arrive?	

A Grammar   *I'm sitting on the balcony*

Links

I'm, we're	➲ 58A
listen, write, play	
	➲ 55B
eat, drink	➲ 42A

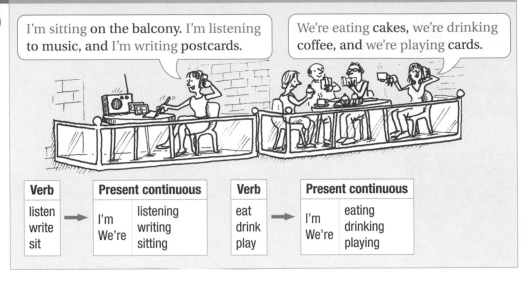

> I'm sitting on the balcony. I'm listening to music, and I'm writing postcards.

> We're eating cakes, we're drinking coffee, and we're playing cards.

Verb		Present continuous
listen	I'm	listening
write	We're	writing
sit		sitting

Verb		Present continuous
eat	I'm	eating
drink	We're	drinking
play		playing

1 Complete the sentences. Use verbs from the tables.

a   I'm sitting _____ in the office.
b   _____ pizza.
c   _____ emails.
d   _____ lemonade.
e   We're _____ on the beach.
f   _____ to the radio.
g   _____ ice cream.
h   _____ chess.

B Grammar   *We're staying with a friend*

> We're staying with a friend in Paris, and we're learning French at a language school.

> I'm living in London now. I'm working in a café for the summer.

PARIS

London

Verb		Present continuous
stay	I'm	staying
learn	We're	learning
work		working
live		living

2 Complete the postcards. Use words from the box.

Links

at ➔ 22A

in the morning, evening ➔ 5C

(a) We're staying _____ in London this summer. (b) _____ English at a language school.

(c) _____ in Berlin now. (d) _____ at the university.

(e) _____ at a small hotel in Madrid. (f) _____ Spanish in the morning, and (g) _____ in a restaurant in the evening.

a	we / stay
b	I / learn
c	we / live
d	we / work
e	I / stay
f	I / learn
g	I / work

C Grammar   *I'm not living there now*

Link

I'm not, we aren't ➔ 59

How's London?

Is your hotel good?

I'm not living in London now. I'm living in Oxford.

We aren't staying at a hotel. We're staying with friends.

| I'm | living staying | ➔ | I'm not | living staying |

| We're | living staying | ➔ | We aren't | living staying |

3 Write sentences. Use **I'm not** or **We aren't**.

a We're living in Zurich, not Geneva.   We aren't living in Geneva.

b I'm learning Russian, not Spanish.   _____

c I'm studying geography, not maths.   _____

d I'm working in a hotel, not a restaurant.   _____

e We're staying at a hotel, not a campsite.   _____

f We're talking about Sue, not Sue's sister.   _____

Verb tables

Present continuous
page 173

Write in your language

I'm learning English.	
We're staying with friends.	
We aren't staying at a hotel.	

Present continuous (2)

He's/She's/They're (reading); He/She isn't (reading), They aren't (reading)

A Grammar — *She's reading a letter*

Links

He's, She's	➔58C
stand, sit	➔49A

A woman **is standing** by a window. **She's reading** a letter. **She's wearing** a long dress.

A man **is sitting** at a table. **He's playing** cards. **He's wearing** a hat, and he's **smoking** a pipe.

Verb		Present continuous
stand read wear	➔	He's She's — standing … reading … wearing …

Verb		Present continuous
sit play smoke	➔	He's She's — sitting … playing … smoking …

1 Write sentences about the people. Use verbs from the tables.

a _She's sitting_____ at a table.
   _____ a book.
   _____ a white dress.
b _He's_____ by the door.
   _____ a guitar.
c _____ by the window.
   _____ a pipe.

B Grammar — *They're talking*

Link

They're …	➔58C

They're in the garden …

… **They're standing** by the swimming pool …

… **They're talking** …

… **They're laughing** …

… and **they're shaking** hands.

Verb		Present continuous
stand talk	➔	they're — standing … talking …

Verb		Present continuous
laugh shake	➔	they're — laughing … shaking …

2 What are the people doing? Write sentences. Use verbs from the box.

a _They're talking._   d _____

b _____   e _____

c _____   f _____

drink	✓ talk
eat	smoke
laugh	read

Link

isn't, aren't   ➲ 59B

C Grammar   *He isn't eating*

Look at the five men in the picture.

A is eating. B isn't eating.

B and E are reading. A, C and D aren't reading.

He She	isn't	eating. reading.

They aren't	eating. reading.

A   B   C   D   E

3 What are the men's names?

Alex is wearing glasses.   John and Nick aren't wearing hats.
Nick isn't eating.   Alex and Bill aren't reading.
Peter isn't talking on the phone.

A _____ B _____ C _____ D _____ E _____

Now complete the sentences.

a Alex _____ a hat.   **d** Bill and Peter _____ glasses.

b Nick _____ a book.   **e** Bill and Peter _____ hats.

c John _____ on the phone.   **f** Peter _____ a sandwich.

Verb tables

Present continuous
page 173

Write in your language

She's standing by the window.	
They're shaking hands.	
He isn't wearing glasses.	

70 Present continuous (3)

Are you ...-ing, Is she ...-ing ...?; Yes, I am, No, I'm not ...; What/Where/Who ...?

A Grammar — *Is the train coming?*

Link
→ 68, 69 **Present continuous (1), (2)**

Link
I, we, you ... → 17

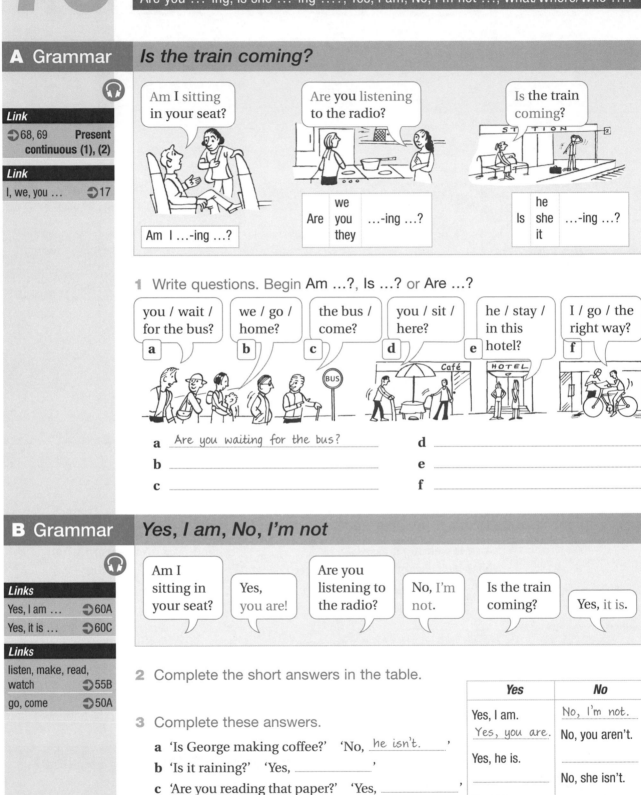

Am I sitting in your seat?

| Am | I | ...-ing ...? |

Are you listening to the radio?

| Are | we you they | ...-ing ...? |

Is the train coming?

| Is | he she it | ...-ing ...? |

1 Write questions. Begin **Am ...?**, **Is ...?** or **Are ...?**

a you / wait / for the bus?
b we / go / home?
c the bus / come?
d you / sit / here?
e he / stay / in this hotel?
f I / go / the right way?

a *Are you waiting for the bus?*
b ....
c ....
d ....
e ....
f ....

B Grammar — *Yes, I am, No, I'm not*

Links
Yes, I am ... → 60A
Yes, it is ... → 60C

Links
listen, make, read, watch → 55B
go, come → 50A

Am I sitting in your seat? Yes, you are!

Are you listening to the radio? No, I'm not.

Is the train coming? Yes, it is.

2 Complete the short answers in the table.

3 Complete these answers.

a 'Is George making coffee?' 'No, *he isn't.* '
b 'Is it raining?' 'Yes, ... ,'
c 'Are you reading that paper?' 'Yes, ... ,'
d 'Are they watching TV?' 'Yes, ... ,'
e 'Is the bus coming?' 'No, ... ,'
f 'Is Maria staying here?' 'Yes, ... ,'

Yes	No
Yes, I am.	No, I'm not.
Yes, you are.	No, you aren't.
Yes, he is.	
	No, she isn't.
Yes, it is.	
	No, we aren't.
Yes, they are.	

Where are you going?

Link
What, Where, Who
⮌79A

What		
What		
Where	am I	...-ing?
Who		

What			
What		we	
Where	are	you	...-ing?
Who		they	

What			
What		he	
Where	is	she	...-ing?
Who			

4 Make questions with **What**, **Where** or **Who**.

a Are you drinking water? Are you drinking milk?   *What are you drinking?*

b Is she studying French? Is she studying Russian?   ....

c Are they watching a film? Are they watching sport?   ....

d Is he working in a shop? Is he working in a café?   ....

e Are you writing to John? Are you writing to Joe?   ....

f Are we going to the cinema? Are we going home?   ....

D Phrases

What are you doing?

5 Make questions with **What ... doing?**

a   *What are you doing?*

   We're playing chess.

b   ....

   He's working.

c   ....

   They're sitting in the garden.

d   ....

   She's reading the paper.

e   ....

   They're watching TV.

f   ....

   I'm having lunch.

Verb tables
Present continuous
page 173

Write in your language

Is the bus coming?	
What is he doing?	
Who are you talking to?	

71 Present continuous (4)

(She's) going/having/playing … (next week); When/Who/Where/How are you …-ing?

A Grammar — *We're going to Crete next summer*

Link
→ 68, 69 **Present continuous (1), (2)**

Link
next, this → 7C

We're going to Crete next summer. We're staying in an apartment in Agios Nikolaos.

Apartment holidays in Crete

We're	going … (next summer)
	staying …

1 Look at the advertisements for summer holidays. Where are the people going this summer? Where are they staying?

a They're going to Scotland.
They're staying in a cottage.

b _____

c _____

d _____

a Stay In a cottage in SCOTLAND

b MIAMI — Luxury holiday apartments

c The Carlton Hotel — Singapore

d Villa Holidays in ITALY

B Grammar — *I'm playing tennis in the evening*

Links
have lunch → 57A
on Monday → 5A
in the evening, on Tuesday morning → 5C, D

… I'm having lunch with a friend on Monday …

… and then I'm playing tennis in the evening …

… and on Tuesday morning I'm going to Manchester …

Monday 7 June	lunch with Paul 12.30 Tennis – 7.00
Tuesday 8 June	Manchester (6.45 train)

I'm	having …
	playing …
	going …

2 Complete the sentences about the woman. Use words from the boxes.

On Wednesday, (a) _she's going to the theatre_ .
On Thursday, (b) _____, and
in the evening, (c) _____ with
a friend. On Friday, (d) _____ .
On Saturday morning, (e) _____,
and then (f) _____ with her
mother. In the evening, (g) _____ .

go	to the sports centre
have	lunch
play	to a party
	dinner
	to Cambridge
	tennis
	to the theatre ✓

C Phrases

Link

➲70 **Present
continuous (3)**

Links

go, come back ➲ 50B
When? Where? Who?
➲79
How? ➲80A

When are you going?

I'm going to Paris next week.

| When are you going? | Who are you going with? | How are you getting there? | Where are you staying? | When are you coming back? |

| On Tuesday. | With Mary. | By train. | At a hotel. | At the weekend. |

---

3 Write the questions.

a
I'm going to Jamaica.

When are you going ?

Next week.

_____ ?

At the end of the month.

b
I'm going to Mike's party tonight.

_____ ?

We're going by taxi.

_____ ?

Jack and Lisa.

c
We're going to Lanzarote this summer.

_____ ?

In July.

_____ ?

In a holiday apartment.

Verb tables

Present continuous
page 173

Write in your language

We're going to London next week.	
They're playing tennis on Tuesday.	
How are you getting there?	

Imperatives

Push, Ring, Wait, Click …; Come in, Sit down …; Don't (eat) …

A Vocabulary Signs

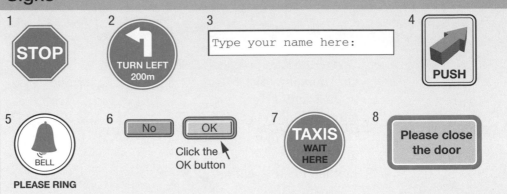

1 Look at the signs. Which can you see …

a in the street?

b in a building?

c on a computer screen?

Verbs		
stop		

Find the verbs and write them in the table.

2 Complete the sentences with verbs from the table. Use each verb once.

a _Wait_ . I'm coming in a minute!

b .... the bell – I know they're at home.

c Just .... the door, and it will open.

d .... The lights are red.

e .... your address and phone number here.

f .... right at the supermarket and go over the bridge.

g .... the window! It's cold!

h .... the 'No' button.

Link

name, address,
phone number ➲ 32C

B Phrases *Come in*

Links

sit down ➲ 49B

look, listen ➲ 52B

Come **in**. Sit **down**. Come **here**. Look **at this**. Listen.

3 Choose the right words.

Open your books at page 12 and (a) *look at* / *listen to* the picture. Now (b) *look at* / *listen to* the CD.

Ah, Mr Cox … (c) *Come in* / *Sit down* and (d) *come in* / *sit down* … Now, what's the problem?

John! … (e) *Come here* / *Sit down* a minute … (f) *Look at* / *Listen to* that. What is it?

C Grammar

Eat fruit, Don't eat sweets

Links

eat, drink, fruit,
vegetables ⮕42

sweets, chocolate,
biscuits ⮕43C

Feel **GOOD** in 10 days!

- ◆ ✓ **Eat** fruit and vegetables.
- ◆ ✗ **Don't eat** sweets, chocolate and biscuits.
- ◆ ✗ **Don't drink** coffee.
- ◆ ✓ **Drink** water and fruit juice.

Yes (positive)	
Eat	…
Drink	

No (negative)	
Don't eat	…
Don't drink	

4 Write positive or negative sentences. Use words from the boxes.

- ◆ ✗ Don't smoke.
- ◆ ✓ Go out with friends.
- ◆ _____
- ◆ _____
- ◆ _____
- ◆ _____
- ◆ _____
- ◆ _____

smoke

go out with friends

go for walks

work at the weekend

 eat late in the evening

 smile a lot

 watch TV every evening

 do sport every week

---

Write in your language

Ring the bell, and open the door.	
Come here and look at this!	
Don't smoke in here, please.	

73 *will* and *won't*

will, won't; I'll, we'll, he'll …; *questions with* will

A Grammar — *will, won't*

Links

| warm, sunny … | ⮕ 38 |
| today, tomorrow | ⮕ 7C |

Today
19°

Tomorrow
15°

Thursday
10°

Today it is warm and sunny.

Tomorrow, it will be cloudy, and it won't be warm.

On Thursday it will be cool, and it will rain.

Now	
It is	warm.
	sunny.

The future		
It	will	be cloudy.
	won't	rain.

won't = will not

1 Look at the weather map for tomorrow. Write **will** or **won't**.

a It _will_ be sunny in Tokyo.

b It _____ rain in Beijing.

c It _____ be warm in Bangkok.

d It _____ rain in Shanghai.

e It _____ be hot in Beijing.

f It _____ be cloudy in Tokyo.

B Grammar — *I'll, we'll, he'll …*

You know about the meeting next Friday, John.
  Yes. I'll be there.
What about Stephen?
  Yes. He'll be there.
And what about Richard and Bob?
  They'll be there.
And Fiona?
  No, she won't be there. She'll be in Paris.

INTEREXPORT INC.

Meeting, London Office
11.30 a.m., Friday 14th Oct.

John	✓ OK
Stephen	✓ OK
Richard	✓ OK
Bob	✓ OK
Fiona	No – in Paris

Positive			Negative
Long form	→	Short form	
I will	→	I'll	I won't
He will	→	He'll	He won't
She will	→	She'll	She won't
They will	→	They'll	They won't

2 Here are some more questions about the meeting. Write the answers.

a What about Alex?

He won't be there. He'll be in New York.

b What about Rex and Max?

....

c What about Salma?

....

d What about Hamid and Sue?

....

e What about Mary?

....

f What about Ali?

....

Alex	No – in New York
Mary	✓ OK
Sue	No ⟍ on holiday
Hamid	No ⟋
Salma	No – in Hong Kong
Rex	✓ OK
Max	✓ OK
Ali	No – on holiday

C Grammar

Will it rain tonight?

Will it **rain** tonight?

No, it won't.

Will you **phone** me tomorrow?

Yes, I will.

Will they **be** at the meeting?

No, they won't.

Sentence	Question	Answer
It will …	Will **it** …?	Yes, **it** will. / No, **it** won't.
I'll …	Will **you** …?	Yes, **I** will. / No, **I** won't.
They'll …	Will **they** …?	Yes, **they** will. / No, **they** won't.

3 Complete the questions and answers.

a _Will_ you write to me?

Yes, I ....

b .... see the Eiffel Tower?

Yes, we ....

c .... be cold tonight?

..............., it won't.

d .... Sue and Hamid be at the meeting?

No, ...

e .... your mother be at home tonight?

.... will.

f .... be at the party?

..............., I won't.

Verb tables

will

page 174

Write in your language

It won't rain on Friday.	
I'll see you tonight.	
Will you be at the meeting tomorrow?	

74 I'll, I won't, Shall I ...?

I'll, I won't; Shall I/we ...?; What/Where shall I ...?

A Grammar | *I'll have an ice cream*

Link

➲73   *will* and *won't*

> I think I'll have a Maxx ...
> No, I won't have a Maxx, I'll
> have a Supremo ... or maybe
> I'll have a Choc Bar ... No, I
> won't have a Choc Bar ...
> Maybe I'll have a Maxx ...

Yes (positive)	**No** (negative)
I'll + *verb*	I won't + *verb*

1 Complete the sentences. Write **I'll** or **I won't**.

  a Look – there's a phone box. _I'll_ _____ just phone my mother.

  b I like this coat. I think _____ buy it.

  c _____ go swimming today. It's cold.

  d _____ come in. My shoes are dirty.

  e _____ buy the food. I have lots of money.

  f _____ have any cake, thanks. I'm not hungry.

B Phrases | *Shall I take an umbrella?*

Links

Shall I ...?   ➲78A

take, buy   ➲ 51

umbrella, wear,
dress   ➲27

Shall I take
an umbrella?

Shall I buy
a newspaper?

Shall I wear my
black dress?

	Sentence			**Question**
I'll	take an umbrella. buy a newspaper. wear my black dress.	→	Shall I	take an umbrella? buy a newspaper? wear my black dress?

158

2 A woman is going to a friend's party. What is she thinking?
Write questions with **Shall I ...?** Use words from the boxes.

Links

| give (her) | ➲51C |
| by car, by taxi | ➲31B |

a _Shall I go by car?_

b ....

c ....

d ....

e ....

f ....

g ....

go	chocolates
give her	by taxi
wear	with John
	earrings
	✓ by car
	a dress
	flowers

C Phrases

Where shall we go?

Link

| What, Where | ➲79A |

Shall we go to Mexico?
Or shall we go to Florida?

Shall I buy apples?
Or shall I buy bananas?

Where shall we **go**?

What shall I **buy**?

| Where
What | shall | I
we | + _verb_ ? |

3 Write questions with **What ...?** or **Where ...?**

Link

| by the window,
on the floor ... | ➲41C |

a Shall I give him _a camera_? Or shall
I give him _a jumper_?

What shall I give him?

b Shall we go _to the theatre_? Or shall
we go _to the cinema_?

....

c Shall I have _spaghetti_? Or shall I
have _pizza_?

....

d Shall we sit _by the window_? Or shall
we sit _by the door_?

....

e Shall I wear _a suit_? Or shall I wear _jeans_?   ....

f Shall I put the bag _on the table_? Or
shall I put it _on the floor_?

....

Write in your language

I think I'll buy a newspaper.	
Shall we go to the party?	
Where shall I put my coat?	

75 can (1)

can/can't …; Can you …?; Yes, I can / No, I can't

A Grammar — *I can, I can't*

***Yes* (positive)**	***No* (negative)**
I can swim.	I can't swim.
I can speak French.	I can't speak French.
I can play the piano.	I can't play the piano.

can't = can not / cannot

❗ I can swim.
NOT ~~I can to swim.~~

1 Write about you.

a ride a motorbike   I can ride a motorbike.   OR   I can't ride a motorbike.

b ride a bike ....   **e** swim ....

c ride a horse ....   **f** speak Arabic ....

d drive a car ....   **g** play the guitar ....

B Grammar — *She can't read*

Links

sit, stand, walk, swim
➲49

read, write, play ➲55B

Lisa is two years old.

She can stand, and
she can walk …

… but she can't
read, and she
can't write.

| She can | stand.
walk. |
|---|---|

| She can't | read.
write. |
|---|---|

2 Write sentences about Lisa. Use **She can** or **She can't**. Use words from
the box.

a   She can sit.

b ....

c ....

d ....

e ....

f ....

✓ sit
drink
drive a car
talk
play chess
ride a horse

160

Can you drive a car?

Can you drive a car?

Yes, I can.

Can you ride a horse?

No, I can't.

What can people in the UK do?

We ask 100 people, age 16–60.

88% can ride a bike.

68% can use a computer.

57% can drive a car.

38% can speak French or German.

23% can play chess.

13% can play the piano.

4% can ride a horse.

Can you	drive a car? ride a horse?	Yes, I can. No, I can't.

3 Look at the people's answers. Write the questions.

Questions

Answers

	0%	25%	50%	75%	100%

a Can you speak French or German?   YES   NO

b _____

c _____

d _____

e _____

f _____

g _____

Look at the questions again. What are your answers?

a Yes, I can.   OR   No, I can't.

b _____

c _____

d _____

e _____

f _____

g _____

Verb tables

can
page 174

Write in your language

I can ride a bike, but I can't ride a horse.	
Can you speak German?	
Yes I can. / No, I can't.	

76 can (2)

A Phrases — *You can …*

Link
→ 75 *can* (1)

In Rio de Janeiro …

… you can **see** the Carnival …

… you can **go** up Sugar Loaf Mountain …

… and you can **visit** Ipanema beach.

1 Write sentences with **You can …** . Use phrases from the box.

a In New York, *you can visit the Empire State Building,*

_____

and _____

b In Venice, _____

and _____

c In Cairo, _____

and _____

> ride in a gondola
> sit by the River Nile
> sit in Piazza San Marco
> ✓ visit the Empire State Building
> visit the Pyramids
> sit in Central Park
> see the Statue of Liberty

B Grammar — *You can't park here*

= You **can** park your car here.

= You **can't** park your car here.

= You **can** drink the water.

= You **can't** drink the water.

| You | can | park your car here. |
| | can't | drink the water. |

162

2 Make sentences with **can** or **can't**. Use phrases from the box.

a   You can put your suitcase here.
....

b   ....

c   ....

d   ....

e   ....

f   ....

g   ....

| swim here |
| take photos here |
| ride a bike here |
| ✓ put your suitcase here |
| smoke here |
| put bottles here |
| use your phone here |

C Phrases

Links

| phone, fax … | ➡32 |
| a, some | ➡15B |

Can I use your phone?

Can I	use your phone?
	have a pen?
	send a fax?

3 You are visiting someone's office. Ask questions with **Can I …?** Use verbs from the box.

| use   have   send |

a   Can I have   some coffee?   d   ....   some paper?

b   ....   your computer?   e   ....   a glass of water?

c   ....   an email?   f   ....   the toilet?

Verb tables

can
page 174

Write in your language

You can visit Central Park.	
You can't use your phone here.	
Can I send a fax?	

Asking for things

Could/Can you ...?; Can I have ...?; I'd like / I'll have ...

A Phrases

Could you ...? Can you ...?

Link

give me, bring me

⮕51C

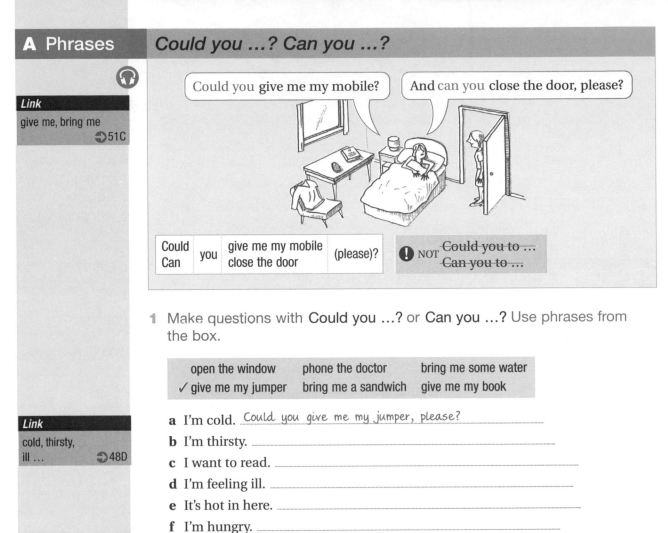

Could you **give me my mobile**?

And can you **close the door, please**?

| Could | you | give me my mobile | (please)? |
| Can | | close the door | |

❗ NOT ~~Could you to ...~~
~~Can you to ...~~

1 Make questions with **Could you ...?** or **Can you ...?** Use phrases from the box.

open the window	phone the doctor	bring me some water
✓ give me my jumper	bring me a sandwich	give me my book

Link

cold, thirsty,
ill ...   ⮕48D

a I'm cold. _Could you give me my jumper, please?_

b I'm thirsty. _____

c I want to read. _____

d I'm feeling ill. _____

e It's hot in here. _____

f I'm hungry. _____

B Phrases

Can I have a newspaper?

Link

⮕76   *can* (2)

On a plane ...

Can I have **a newspaper, please**?

In a restaurant ...

Could I have **some water, please**?

| Can | I have | a newspaper | (please)? |
| Could | | some water | |

2 Which things do you ask for in a restaurant? Which things do you ask for on a plane? Write R or P.

R a knife   ☐ a pillow   ☐ an ashtray   ☐ the menu

☐ a blanket   ☐ the bill   ☐ a magazine

Write questions with **Can I have …?** or **Could I have …?**

	In a restaurant		On a plane
a	Can I have a knife, please?	**e**	
b		**f**	
c		**g**	
d			

C Phrases

I'll have, I'd like

Link
➔42, 43 **Food and drink (1), (2)**

Link
I'd like ➔54C

Links
(like)s, doesn't (like) ➔65A, B
never ➔9B

I'll have burger and chips, please.

And I'd like kebabs with salad.

3 Four friends go to a restaurant.

- John likes meat, but he doesn't like fish, salad or tomatoes.
- Laura never eats green vegetables, and she doesn't like chicken.
- Hamid doesn't eat meat or fish.
- Fatima doesn't eat rice or potatoes, and she doesn't like soup.

What do they ask for? Make sentences with **I'd like** or **I'll have**.

John — I'll have chicken soup, and then I'd like chicken with rice, please.

Laura —

Hamid —

Fatima —

Lunch Menu

Starters
Salad with fish
Chicken soup
Tomato soup

Main dishes
Chicken with rice
Fish with potatoes
Chicken and salad
Green beans with potatoes and tomatoes

Write in your language

Could you close the window?	
Can I have the bill, please?	
I'll have chicken and chips, please.	

78 Offers and suggestions

Shall I …?; Would you like (to) …? ; Let's / Shall we …

A Phrases

Shall I …?

Links

→ 74   **I'll, I won't, Shall I…?**

at   → 22A

At an airport …

> Shall I **get** a trolley?

At a restaurant …

> Shall I **take** your coat?

At home …

> Shall I **wash** the dishes?

Shall I	get a trolley?
	take your coat?
	wash the dishes?

1   Write more questions with **Shall I …?** Use phrases from the box.

At an airport	**a**	Shall I carry your suitcase?
	b	
At a restaurant	**c**	
	d	
At home	**e**	
	f	

open the window
✓ carry your suitcase
call the waiter
buy some sandwiches
ask for the bill
make some coffee

B Grammar

Would you like (to) …?

Link

would like (to)   → 54C

A friend is staying at John's house. Read the conversations.

John   Would you like **a cup of coffee?**
Friend   Yes, please.

John   Would you like to **have a shower?**
Friend   No, thanks.

would you like + noun	
Would you like	a cup of coffee?
	a sandwich?

would you like to + verb	
Would you like to	have a shower?
	use my car?

2   Make questions with **Would you like …?** or **Would you like to …?**

a	Would you like	an apple?	**e**		read the paper?
b		watch TV?	**f**		some chocolate?
c		a drink?	**g**		see my holiday
d		use my computer?			photos?

Shall we …?, Let's …

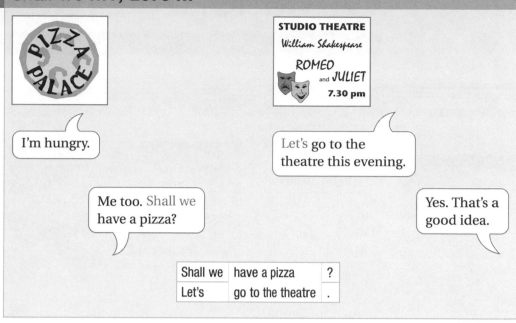

3 Write suggestions with **Shall we** or **Let's**. Use phrases from the box.

| go for a walk | go to the cinema | go shopping |
| go swimming | go to a restaurant | ✓go to a concert |

Link

go to, go for,
go …-ing ➡50C

a Let's go to a concert.

b

c

d

e

f

a Boston Symphony Orchestra
Mozart: Requiem

b HOCHBERG 15km

c LA FONTANA — The best in Italian cooking

d SWIMMING POOL Opening hours: 8.00–16.00

e ASHBURY PLAZA — PC CENTRE Computers — KIDS' CLOTHES — SOUNDS Music superstore

f CINE MAXX Tonight's film: House of the Dead 18.00 20.00 22.00

Write in your language

Shall I take you to the airport?	
Would you like to go to the theatre?	
Let's watch TV.	

79 Question words (1)

Who …?, What …?, Where …?; When / What time …?; What (music) do you like?

A Phrases — Who? What? Where?

Links

that	13A
Who?, What?, Where?	60D

Where's that?

It's the Antarctic.

Who's that?

Ernest Shackleton.

What's that?

It's a penguin!

Who's	
What's	that?
Where's	

1 Ask questions. Use **Who**, **What** or **Where**.

a — Where's that?
It's Brussels.

b —
The Atomium.

c —
It's the South Pole.

d —
Roald Amundsen.

e —
George Harrison.

f —
It's a sitar.

B Phrases — Questions with What …?

Links

name, address, phone number	32C
day, month	7A
weather	38A

What's **your address**?

102, London Road, Bristol.

What **day** is it?

Monday.

What's **John** like?

He's very nice.

What's	your name? your address? your phone number?

What	time day month	is it?

What's	the weather London John	like?

2 Ask questions from the tables.

a — What's your name?
Alex.

b —
675 87695.

c —
It's cold.

d —
August.

e —
He's very friendly.

f —
About three o'clock.

C Phrases — Where? When? What time?

Links

on 5th May	➲2C
at 8.00	➲4B
on Sunday	➲5A

Where **is** the concert?
It's at the City Hall.

When **is** the concert?
It's on 14th November.

What time **is** the concert?
It's at seven o'clock.

CONCERT
City Hall
14 November
7.00 pm

3 Write questions. Use **Where**, **When** or **What time**.

a *Where is the flower show?*
It's in Queen's Park.

b ....
It's on 5th May.

c ....
It's in Room 503.

d ....
It's at 12.00.

e ....
It's on Sunday.

f ....
It's at 8.00.

Flower Show
Queen's Park
Sunday 1st June
Tickets £5

MEETING
Monday 5 April
at 12.00
in Room 503

Come to our
PARTY
on: *Friday 5th May*
at: *8 o'clock*
at: *Mary's house*

D Phrases — What music do you like?

Link

Do you ...?	➲66A

Do you like Beethoven? Do you like jazz? ➜ What music **do you like?**

Do you like coffee? Do you like pineapple juice? ➜ What drinks **do you like?**

What	music / drinks	do you like?

4 Write questions. Use words from the box.

writers   colours   ✓food   football teams   fruit   sports

a Do you like *cheese*? Do you like *fish*?   *What food do you like?*

b Do you like *golf*? Do you like *tennis*?   ....

c Do you like *Real Madrid*? Do you like *Arsenal*?   ....

d Do you like *red*? Do you like *green*?   ....

e Do you like *Tolstoy*? Do you like *Dostoyevsky*?   ....

f Do you like *oranges*? Do you like *apples*?   ....

Write in your language

What's the weather like?	
What time is the concert?	
What sports do you like?	

Question words (2)

How ...? How far ...? How much ...? How old ...?; Why ...?

A Phrases

How? How far? How much?

How **can** I get to the airport?
  You can go by bus, or by boat.
How **far** is it?
  About 20 kilometres.
How **much** is it by boat?
  25 euros.

How	can I get to ...?
	do I get to ...?

How far	is it?
How much	

1 Complete the questions.

a _____ get to the Lido?
  You can go by boat.
  _____ is it?
  About five euros.

c _____ the station?
  Go straight along this street.
  _____?
  About 200 metres.

b _____ to Mestre?
  About ten kilometres.
  _____ get there?
  By train or by bus.

d _____ Verona?
  By train or by bus.
  _____ by train?
  About 20 euros.

B Phrases

How are you? How old are you?

Hi. **How** are you?

I'm fine, thanks.

How old are you?

I'm six.

How is your mother?

Oh, she's not too bad.

How old are your children?

One's 16, and one's 14.

How	are you?
	is your mother?

How old	are you?
	are your children?

2 Write questions with **How …?** or **How old …?** Use words from the box.

Link

brother, sister …

➲28A

a <u>How is your brother?</u>

He's OK. He's working now.

b _____

I'm OK, thanks.

c _____

They're both over 80.

d _____

They're fine. They're at school now.

e _____

She's nearly three.

f _____

It's about 150 years old.

your sister	your children
✓ your brother	your house
your parents	you

C Phrases

Why?

| Why | is the shop closed? / are you wearing a hat? | Because … |

❗ NOT ~~Why the shop is closed? , Why you are wearing a hat?~~

3 Write questions. Then match them with the answers in the box.

a The plane is late.

<u>Why is the plane late?</u> [4]

b She's having a party.

_____ [ ]

c She's learning Japanese.

_____ [ ]

d He's running.

_____ [ ]

e He's always tired.

_____ [ ]

f The room is cold.

_____ [ ]

1 Because he goes to bed late.
2 Because she's going to Tokyo next year.
3 Because he's late for work.
✓4 Because the weather's bad.
5 Because the window's open.
6 Because it's her birthday.

Write in your language

How far is it to the station?	
How are your parents?	
Why are the shops closed today?	

Verb tables

Positive

Full form		Short form
I am		I'm
You are		You're
He/She is		He's/She's
It is		It's
We are		We're
They are		They're

Negative

I'm not		–
You're not		You aren't
He's/She's not		He/She isn't
It's not	OR	It isn't
We're not		We aren't
They're not		They aren't

Questions and Short answers

Am I			I am.		I'm not.
Are you			you are.		you aren't.
Is he/she	…?	Yes,	he/she is.	No,	he/she isn't.
Is it			it is.		it is.
Are we			we are.		we aren't.
Are they			they are.		they aren't.

Wh- questions

	am I?
	are you?
Where	is he/she?
	is it?
	are we?
	are they?

Positive

There is (There's)	a shop. a man in the room.

There are	lots of shops. two men in the room.

Negative

There isn't	a shop. a man in the room.

There aren't	any shops. any people in the room.

Questions and Short answers

Is there a shop near here?	Yes, there is. No, there isn't.

Are there any shops near here?	Yes, there are. No, there aren't.

Wh- questions

How many	shops people	are there?

Present simple
Units 63, 64, 65, 66, 67

Positive

I You We They	live go have		He She It	lives goes has

Negative

I You We They	don't	live go have		He She It	doesn't	live go have

Questions and Short answers

Do	I you we they	live …? go …? have …?		Yes,	I you we they	do.		No,	I you we they	don't.

Does	he she it	live …? go …? have …?		Yes,	he she it	does.		No,	he she it	doesn't.

Wh- questions

Where do	I you we they	live?

Where does	he she it	live?

-s endings

Verb + -s		Verb + -es		-y → -ies		Irregular	
work	→ works	go	→ goes	study	→ studies	have	→ has
live	→ lives	watch	→ watches				

Present continuous
Units 68, 69, 70, 71

Positive

I'm You're He's/She's It's We're They're	going.

Negative

I'm not You aren't He/She isn't It isn't We aren't They aren't	going.

Questions and Short answers

Am I Are you Is he/she Is it Are we Are they	going?		Yes,	I am. you are. he/she is. it is. we are. they are.		No,	I'm not. you aren't. he/she isn't. it isn't. we aren't. they aren't.

Wh- questions

Where When	am I are you is he/she is it are we are they	going?

-ing forms

listen	→ listening	write	→ writing	sit	→ sitting
eat	→ eating	live	→ living	run	→ running
go	→ going	smoke	→ smoking	swim	→ swimming
play	→ playing	come	→ coming		
do	→ doing	have	→ having		

Positive

Full form		
I You He/She It We They	will	go.

Short form	
I'll You'll He'll/She'll It'll We'll They'll	go.

Negative

I You He/She It We They	will not won't	go.

Questions and Short answers

Will	I you he/she it we they	go?

Yes,	I you he/she it	will.
No,	we they	won't.

Wh- questions

When Where How	will	I you he/she it we they	go?

Positive and Negative

I You He/She It We They	can can't	swim.

Questions and Short answers

Can	I you he/she it we they	swim?

Yes,	I you he/she it	can.
No,	we they	can't.

Answer key

1 Numbers (1)

1

2
b eleven
c twelve
d fifteen
e nineteen
f fourteen

3
b fifty-one, fifty-three
c eighty-nine, eighty-eight
d fifty-nine, sixty
e thirty-eight, thirty-six

4
b forty-five
c forty-eight
d thirty-six
e sixty-seven
f twenty-four; ninety-nine

5
b two thousand
c fifty thousand
d five million
e three thousand
f a million
g six hundred and fifty

2 Numbers (2)

1
a seventh
b eighteenth
c fifteenth
d first, second, third

2
b on the second floor
c on the fifteenth floor
d on the eighth floor
e on the thirteenth floor
f on the sixth floor
g on the sixteenth floor

3
b the twenty-ninth of May (29th May).
c On the fourteenth of June (14th June).
d On the twelfth of June (12th June).
e On the twenty-seventh of May (27th May).
f On the sixth of June (6th June).

3 Time (1)

1
b It's one o'clock
c It's three o'clock
d It's nine o'clock
e It's eight o'clock
f It's ten o'clock

2
b It's half past seven.   4
c It's quarter to five.   5
d It's quarter past ten.   1
e It's half past twelve.   2

3
b five to six
c twenty-five past ten
d ten to nine
e twenty to three

4
b What time is it? It's about quarter to two.
c What time is it? It's twenty past five.
d What's the time? It's about seven o'clock.

4 Time (2)

1
b half past nine; nine thirty
c twenty-five to six; five thirty-five
d quarter past four; four fifteen
e twenty past nine; nine twenty

2
a at five fifteen
b at five o'clock; at seven thirty
c at eight o'clock; at five thirty
d at six forty-five; at eleven o'clock

3
b at six thirty in the morning
c at seven thirty in the morning
d at four fifty in the afternoon
e at three forty in the afternoon
f at eleven thirty in the morning

4
b after work
c before dinner
d after breakfast
e after lunch
f before breakfast

5 Days

1
b on Friday
c on Monday
d at the weekend / on Saturday
e on Tuesday
f on Thursday

2

b every Wednesday
c every Sunday / every weekend
d every day
e every Friday
f every weekend

3

Nick	Bob	Lynne	John
Bill	Mary	Ali	Carlos
	Sue	Steve	

b works at night
c works in the evening
d works in the afternoon
e works in the afternoon
f works in the morning

4

b on Saturday evening
c on Friday morning
d on Wednesday evening
e on Monday morning
f on Sunday afternoon

6 Months and seasons

1

b November
c June
d August
e December, January
f May, June

2

b in May
c in October
d in February
e in August
f in July
g in April

3

b I'm getting married in the autumn.
c They're going to England in the spring.
d Greece is very hot in the summer.
e We go skiing in the winter.
f It's quite warm here in the spring.

4

7 Time phrases

1

b weeks; a year
c days; a month
d months; a year
e days; a week

2

b 4
c 2
d 1
e 5
f 3

4

b tomorrow afternoon
c this morning
d this evening (tonight)
e this afternoon
f tomorrow night (tomorrow evening)
g tomorrow morning

8 Age

1

b fifty years old
c twelve years old
d ninety years old
e three years old
f eighteen years old

2

b about 30
c over 100
d about 60
e nearly 20
f over 40

4

b ten months old
c six weeks old
d three days old
e 4,500 years old
f 100 years old

5

b How old are your parents?
c How old is your sister?
d How old are you?
e How old is your house?

9 Frequency

1

b They don't often watch television.
c He often reads in the evening.
d We often go out on Saturday.
e I don't often see my father.
f She doesn't often wear jeans.

2

b I often drink water. / I don't often drink water.
c I often go to the cinema. / I don't often go to the cinema.
d I often wear black clothes. / I don't often wear black clothes.
e I often watch television. / I don't often watch television.

3

Possible answers

b I never listen to music in bed.
c I always sleep with the window open.
d I sometimes sleep with the door open.
e I sometimes wake up in the night.
f I always go to sleep before 12.00.
g I never get up after 8.00.

4

b always wears
c usually wears
d never wears
e usually wears
f always wears

10 Singular and plural

1
b chairs
c plate
d plates
e bowls
f spoons
g bottles
h flowers
i CD player

2
forks; photos; combs; plates; taxis
buses; glasses; brushes; matches
lorries
knives

3
c dresses
d nurses
e secretaries
f churches
g wives
h letters
i watches
j faxes
k shops
l babies

4
b women
c boys
d girls
e children
f people

5
b taxies taxis
c dictionary's dictionaries
d childrens children
e shelfs shelves
f knifes knives
g boxs boxes
h peoples people; photoes photos

11 *a, an, some*

1
a hat, a tree, a man, a banana
an umbrella, an egg, an apple, an orange

2
b a dog
c an antelope
d an octopus
e a horse
f an iguana

3
a … an Italian ice cream
b a young woman in an expensive car
c an old man with a black umbrella
d a Japanese newspaper and an English book

4
a –
b an; –
c –; a
d –; a

5
b a T-shirt
c some jeans
d some eggs
e a newspaper
f some potatoes
g an umbrella

12 *the*

1
b 1
c 3
d 4
e 6
f 5

2
b some; a
c the; the
d the; the
e the

3
b a
c a
d The
e the
f a
g a
h The
i a
j a
k a
l a
m the
n a

4
c –
d –
e the
f the
g The
h –
i the
j –
k the

13 *this, that, these, those*

1
b those/these are
c This is
d that's / this is
e This is
f that's
g those are

2
b this
c these
d that
e These
f those

3
b That's wonderful.
c That's OK.
d that's terrible
e That's a good idea.
f That's right.

14 Countable and uncountable nouns

1
Countable: dogs, a hat, trees, books
Uncountable: lemonade, music, milk, hair, grass

2
b music
c a clock
d hair
e milk
f grass
g an apple
h money

3

b Would you like a cup of coffee?

c There's a bottle of lemonade in the fridge.

d Would you like a glass of orange juice?

e There's a bottle of olive oil in the cupboard.

f There's a bowl of sugar on the table.

15 *some* and *any*

1

b some trees

c a boat

d some people

e some horses

f a bridge

2

b some

c some

d some

e a

f a

3

c ✓

d There isn't any coffee.

e There aren't any cushions.

f There are some curtains.

g ✓

h There aren't any magazines.

16 *a lot, much, many*

1

b She doesn't travel much.

c He reads a lot.

d He doesn't work much.

e She doesn't sleep much.

f It costs a lot.

2

b He doesn't eat much.

c She doesn't sleep much.

d It doesn't cost much.

e She travels a lot.

f He reads a lot.

3

b a lot of

c a lot of

d much

e a lot of

f a lot of

g much

h many

Person 2 has a healthy diet.

4

b How many oranges do we need?

c How much cheese do we need?

d How much butter do we need?

e How many eggs do we need?

f How much sugar do we need?

17 Pronouns (1)

1

a I

b you; We

c you; I

d I; I; you

2

b It's in Rome.

c It's in Colombia.

d She's a tennis player.

e He's a film star.

f They're football teams.

g They're mountains.

3

b ... They teach at the university.

c ... He is 15, and he is still at school.

d ... She is a student. She studies French.

e ... It is very old.

f ... They live in Rome.

18 Pronouns (2)

1

b me

c us

d you

e you

f me

g us

2

b I like him.

c I can't see them.

d I'm seeing them tonight.

e I know him.

f Can you see her?

3

b them

c it

d it

e it

f them

4

a it; It

b them; They; them

c her; She

d He; him; he; me

19 *my, your, his, their ...*

1

b ... My name's Peter. What's your name?

c Here's our address ...

d ... What's your email address?
   ... And my mobile number is ...

e ... Our son is 18 and our daughter is 16.

f ... is this your phone?

2

b their

c her

d his

e their

f his

3

b Ami's

c Kimiko's

d Her brother's

e Her brother's

f Nina's

20 Place prepositions (1)

1
b on
c under
d under
e in
f in
g under
h over

2
b in the cupboard by the window
c on the table by the door
d on the table by the window
e under the chair by the door
f on the shelf by the door

3
b 5 in; on
c 6 in; on
d 2 on; in
e 3 in; in
f 1 on; in

21 Place prepositions (2)

1
a Nat
b Lily
c George
d Frieda
e William
f Albert
g Victoria
h Daniel
i John
j David

2
b is standing behind
c is standing next to / beside
d is sitting between
e is standing behind

3
b It's near the railway station.
c It's opposite the bus station.
d It's opposite the cinema.
e It's next to the cinema.
f It's near the bus station.

4
b above
c above
d below
e above
f below
g above

22 *at* and *to*

1
b at the bus stop
c at the swimming pool
d at a hotel
e at the cinema
f at a football match

2
b They're staying at the Astor Hotel.
c I'm standing at the bus stop.
d Are you going to the football match?
e There's a café at the station.
f I'm going to the airport now.

3
c ✓
d Max is at work in the afternoon . / Max is at home in the morning.
e Teresa is at school in the morning. / Teresa is at home in the afternoon.
f ✓
g Max goes to work at 12.00.

23 Direction prepositions

1
b off the bed … and put them in the cupboard
c out of the car … and put it in the fridge
d off the chair … and put it on the shelf
e out of the cupboard … and put them on the table
f out of the oven … and put them on a plate

2
b into
c out of
d onto
e off
f onto
g out of
h into

3
b through
c up
d through
e down
f across
g along
h across
i across
j down
k along
l under

4
b 4 up
c 7 across/over
d 1 down
e 3 along
f 2 into/through
g 6 under

24 Giving directions

1
b the way to the station
c get to the bus station
d you tell me the way to the cinema
e do I get to the hospital

2
b right
c along/down
d left
e straight
f Go along/down
g turn right
h turn right
i go straight on

3

b Go past

c Turn left at

d Go past the café and turn right.

e Turn left at the traffic lights.

f Go past the cinema and turn left.

25 People

1

(man); woman

teenager

boy; girl

baby

2

a tall

b long; fair, black, grey

c blue, brown

3

a fair hair; green eyes

b is quite short. He has (long) black hair and brown eyes.

4

b 6 a girl with a dog

c 10 a woman with long, black hair

d 8 a man with a long beard

e 1 a man with an umbrella

f 2 an old woman with glasses

26 The body

1

b ears

c hair

d nose

e mouth

f eyes

2

a large eyes; a large nose; small ears; a large mouth

b a long, thin face; large eyes; a small nose; large ears; a small mouth

3

b arm

c hand

d leg

e neck

f tail

g head

h foot

i wing

j leg

4

b 1

c 3

d 6

e 5

f 2

27 Clothes

1

b a dress

c a skirt; a top

d jeans; a T-shirt

e a jacket; trousers

f a coat; a hat

g a jumper; a shirt

2

a He's carrying an umbrella.

b She's wearing a dress. She's carrying a bag.

c She's wearing a coat. She's carrying a suitcase.

d He's wearing glasses.

3

b Take off

c get dressed

d take off

e get undressed

f Put on

28 The family

1

b parents

c father

d wife

e daughter

g daughter

h son

i sister

j mother

k sister

2

… daughter

brother …

husband …

3

b 5

c 8

d 3

e 1

f 4

29 Work

1

c works in a hotel

d works in a school

e works in a hospital

f works in a shop

g works in a restaurant

h works in a hospital

2

b waiter, waitress

c receptionist

d nurse, doctor

e shop assistant

f teacher

3

b He works for Language Direct.

c She works for Baileys.

d He works for Plaza International.

e She works for Gourmets.

f He works for SaveCo.

4

b What do you; I work for

c do you work; I work in

d do you do; I'm a

30 Sport and leisure

1

b He plays golf.

c He plays table tennis.

d He watches football.

e He watches basketball.

f He plays tennis.

3

b go running

c when you go dancing

d when you go walking

e when you go skiing

f when you go
swimming

4

The girl in the picture is
Angie.

b She doesn't play the
guitar.

c She plays cards.

d She doesn't play
computer games.

e She doesn't play chess.

31 Transport

1

b on a bike

c on a bus

d on a boat

e on a train

f in a car

2

b goes by taxi

c goes by car

d goes by bus

e goes by plane

f goes by bike

4

b leaves

c arrives in / gets to

d leaves

e leaves

f leaves

g arrives in / gets to

h arrives in / gets to

32 Communicating

1

b a text / a text message

c a letter

d an email

e a fax

2

b Write to them. / Send
them a letter.

c Email her. / Send her
an email.

d Fax her. / Send her a
fax.

e Write to him. / Send
him a letter.

f Phone/Call him.

3

b email address

c address

d address

e mobile number

f fax number

4

b Can I use your fax
machine?

c Can I use your
computer?

d Can I use your
photocopier?

e Can I use your
phone/mobile?

f Can I use your mobile?

33 Money

1

b one dollar forty

c fourteen pounds
ninety-nine

d four euros fifty

e three dollars twenty

f one pound eighty-five

2

b costs about ten dollars.

c costs about a hundred
dollars.

d costs about fifty
dollars.

e costs about six
hundred dollars.

f costs about forty
dollars.

4

b How much do these
sunglasses cost / are
these sunglasses?

c How much is this bag /
does this bag cost?

d How much does this
shirt cost / is this shirt?

e How much is this
camera / does this
camera cost?

f How much are these
trainers / do these
trainers cost?

5

b He earns € 72,000 a
year.

c She earns € 750 a week.

d He earns € 100 a day.

e She earns € 1,800 a
month.

f He earns € 48,000 a
year.

34 Shops and shopping

1

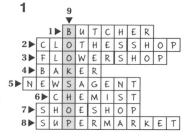

2

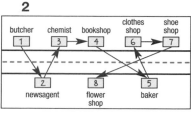

3

b I'd like some apples,
please. / Can I have
some apples please?

c Can I have a baguette,
please? / I'd like a
baguette, please.

d I'd like a large chicken,
please. / Can I have a
large chicken, please.

e Can I have six roses,
please? / I'd like six
roses, please.

f I'd like an ice cream,
please. / Can I have an
ice cream, please?

4

b open

c open

d opens

e closed

f closes

35 Towns

1
b banks
c (railway) station
d library
e cafés
f restaurants
g sports centre

2
b at a hotel
c at a swimming pool
d at a car park
e at a post office
f at a cinema

3
b Where's the bus station?
c Where's the post office?
d Where's the cinema?
e Where's the restaurant?
f Where's the church?

4
b 1
c 2
d 1
e 1
f 1
g 2

36 The countryside

1
a 2
b 6
c 4

2
b along the fence
c through the gate
d across the field
e through the wood
f up the hill

3
b cows
c dog
d sheep; grass
e bird
f horse
g flowers; tree

4

b bird
c fence; wall
d bridge
e river; stream
f sheep; cow; dog; horse
g flowers; tree; grass
You can see all these things in the *countryside*.

37 Natural features

1
b forests
c rivers
d islands
e beaches
f sea
g mountains
h lakes

3
b No. It's on the coast / on the sea.
c No. It's on the sea / on the coast.
d No. It's on a lake.
e No. It's on a river.
f No. It's in the mountains.

4
b in the north of; in the centre of
c in the south of
d in the west of
e in the centre of

38 Weather

1

2
b It's very hot
c It's cool
d It's very cold
e It's warm
f It's hot
g It's cool
h It's cold

3
b it's cold and it's sunny
c it's warm and it's raining
d it's cold and it's snowing
e it's hot and it's sunny
f it's warm and it's cloudy
g it's cool and it's sunny

39 Countries, nationalities, languages

1
Japanese …
… Germany
Italian …
… China
Russian …
… Spain
Brazilian …
… Egypt

2
b We're from France.
c Are you from Russia?
d His wife is Brazilian.
e She's Italian.
f They're American.
g Are they from Britain?
h He isn't Chinese. He's Japanese.

3
b ~~British~~ French
c ~~Brazil~~ Egypt
d ~~Chinese~~ German
e ~~Spanish~~ Italian
f ~~German~~ Russian

4

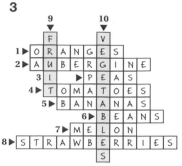

1▶ I T A L I A N
2▶ J A P A N E S E
3▶ C H I N E S E
4▶ G E R M A N
5▶ R U S S I A N
6▶ A R A B I C
7▶ E N G L I S H
8▶ F R E N C H
9▶ S P A N I S H

40 Things

1

b 3
c 5
d 1
e 4
f 2

2

b a key
c a passport
d a pen
e a watch
f money; a credit card

3

c a mirror
d pictures
e a television
f a radio
g books
h a lamp
i plants
j magazines
k a newspaper
l cushions

4

b cushions
c a mirror
d books
e a lamp
f a newspaper
g a radio

5

C R E D I T C A R D
U N E W S P A P E R
S C O M P U T E R P
H C W O X R I N G B
I O A N W A T C H R
O M L E C H A I R U
N B L Y F L O O R S
Y M A G A Z I N E H

a credit card
b newspaper; magazine
c pen; computer
d floor; wall
e ring; watch
f comb; brush
g cushion; chair

41 Rooms and furniture

1

b kitchen
c This is the balcony.
d This is the living room.
e This is the bathroom.
f This is the bedroom.

2

Study: a desk
Kitchen: a fridge; a table; chairs
Living room: a sofa; a TV; shelves
Bathroom: a shower; a bath; a toilet
Bedroom: a bed; a chair; a cupboard
Balcony: a table; chairs

3

b in the corner
c by the window
d on the wall
e by the door
f on the floor

42 Food and drink (1)

1

c She eats fruit every day.
d She never eats meat.
e She never drinks milk.
f She eats vegetables every day.
g She drinks water every day.

3

9   10
F   V
1▶ O R A N G E S
2▶ A U B E R G I N E
3▶ I ▶ P E A S
4▶ T O M A T O E S
5▶ B A N A N A S
6▶ B E A N S
7▶ M E L O N
8▶ S T R A W B E R R I E S
S

5

b three litres of milk
c half a kilo of cheese
d two litres of water
e a kilo of onions
f half a kilo of fish

43 Food and drink (2)

1

b 5 sandwich; soup
c 1 kebabs; rice
d 3 burger; pizza
e 2 steak; chips; salad

2

b French food
c American restaurant
d Chinese food
e Spanish food
f Chinese restaurant
g Italian food

3

ice cream	✓	✓	–
cake	✓	✓	✓
chocolate	✓	✓	–

b She can eat sweets.
c She can eat crisps, sweets, ice cream and chocolate.

44 Meals

1

b have dinner
c have lunch
d have dinner
e have lunch
f have breakfast

2

b having eggs and coffee for breakfast
c having chicken and chips for lunch
d having pizza for dinner
e having spaghetti bolognese for dinner
f having soup for lunch

3

b a knife and fork
c salt and pepper
d a plate and a glass
e a bowl and a spoon
f a plate and chopsticks

4

b 4
c 5
d 2
e 1
f 3

45 Adjectives (1)

1

b an old house
c a cheap coat
d a large nose
e hot water
f dirty shoes
g a small car
h cold weather

2

b old; expensive
c small; young
d good; expensive
e cold; bad

3

b very cold
c very old
d quite old
e very expensive
f quite expensive

4

b very small
c quite big
d very big
e very old
f quite cheap

46 Adjectives (2)

1

b is quite good
c are wonderful/great/ excellent
d are usually very good/ really good
e is awful/terrible
f is really bad/very bad
g is very good/really good
h is wonderful/great/ excellent
i is not very good
j is quite good
k are awful/terrible

2

b a nice time
c a lovely photo
d a lovely day
e a lovely house
f very nice people

3

b uncomfortable
c unfriendly
d interesting
e friendly
f boring

47 Colours

1

b black; white
c red; yellow; green
d white; yellow
e yellow; black
f red; white; blue

2

3

b She's wearing an orange dress.
c They have a black and white cat.

d The Brazilian flag is yellow and green / green and yellow
e Her hair is brown and her eyes are blue.
f She drives a green car.
g I'd like six white roses, please.

4

b What colour is their new car?
c What colour is their cat?
d What colour are British passports?
e What colour is the Japanese flag?
f What colour are her eyes?

48 *Hello, how are you?*

1

b Good morning
c Good night
d Bye
e Good evening
f Hello

2

a Thank you
b Excuse me; sorry
c Excuse me; Thank you; That's all right
d Excuse me; Sorry; Thank you

3

a She's OK / She's not bad
b How are; I'm fine
c How are; They're OK / They're not bad (thanks)
d How is; He's fine (thanks)

4

b 4
c 6
d 3
e 1
f 2

49 stand, sit, lie ...

1
b 4
c 3
d 12
e 2
f 9

2
b 1 She's standing
c 11 He's sitting
d 10 She's lying
e 8 She's standing
f 5 She's sitting

3
b sit down
c lie down
d Stand up
e sit down
f Stand up

4
b jump
c climb
d walk
e climb
f swim
g climb
h run

5
b Lie down.
c Stand up.
d Walk round the room.
e Climb on the box.
f Jump off the box.
g Run round the room.

50 go and come

1
b 7
c 2
d 6
e 3

2
b 9 They're going into
c 8 He's coming out of
d 1 He's going into
e 4 He's coming out of

3
b He's coming back from Budapest
c He's going to Frankfurt
d He's going to Brazil
e He's coming back from Japan
f He's going to Scotland

4
go to a concert, go to the park
go for a drive, go for a drink, go for a meal
go skiing, go swimming

5
a go to the cinema
b go for a drive
c go skiing
d go for a drink
e go shopping
f go to a concert

51 bring, take, get ...

1
b bring
c bring
d take
e taking
f bringing

2
b Take; put
c take
d Take; put
e Put

3
b Could you buy me
c Could you bring me
d Could you buy me
e Could you give me
f Could you give me

4
b bring
c buy
d buy
e bring
f buy

52 Seeing and hearing

1
You can see: traffic, the sea, mountains
You can hear: the wind, traffic, music, the sea

2
a I can hear
b I can hear
c I can see
d I can see
e I can see; I can hear

3
look at: people, a picture
watch: a football match, TV
listen to: the radio, music

4
c ~~looks at~~ listens to
d ~~look at~~ watch
e ~~listen to~~ look at
f ✓
g ✓

5
b looking for
c looking at
d looking for
e looking at
f looking for

53 Saying and thinking

1
b say   e Tell
c Tell   f Tell
d say

2
b talking about music
c talking about clothes
d talking to her father
e talking to her children
f talking about football

3
a answer
b ask; a question
c answers
d answer; question
e ask; questions; answers

4
b I think it's milk. I don't think it's a flower.
c I think it's a fork. I don't think it's a chair.
d I don't think it's hair. I think it's pasta.

54 *want, would like, need*

1
b I want to buy a newspaper.
c She wants to work in the USA.
d I want a drink.
e He wants a CD player.
f I want to see a doctor.
g I want a sandwich.

2
b don't want to
c want to
d want to
e don't want to
f want to
g don't want to
Three people go to Maxie's café.

3
b I'd like to
c I'd like
d I'd like to
e I'd like to
f I'd like
g I'd like
h I'd like to

4
a sugar
b You need a towel.
You need sun cream.
c You need dollars.
You need a passport.
d You need tomatoes.
You need onions.

55 Everyday activities

1
a She wakes up
c She goes to work
d She starts work
f She finishes work
g She gets home
i She has dinner
j She goes to bed
k She goes to sleep

3
b She's watching
c She's washing
d He's making
e He's writing
f They're playing
g She's reading
h She's writing
i He's washing/cleaning
j He's playing

4
b watch
c make; make
d read
e clean
f write

56 *have* (1)

1
b We have a computer.
c My son has a dog.
d My daughter has a bike.
e I have an old car.
f We have a flat in London.

3
b have
c don't have
d doesn't have
e has
f doesn't have

4
b Do you have a watch?
c Do you have a pen?
d Do you have any money?
e Do you have a computer?
f Do you have any water?
g Do you have a mobile?
h Do you have a key?

57 *have* (2)

1
b have lunch
c has a burger
d have an ice cream
e has breakfast
f have a pizza

2
b have a bath
c has a meeting
d has a party
e have a swim
f have a shower

3
b They're having a meal.
c She's having a shower.
d They're having a party.
e He's having a bath.
f She's having an ice cream.

4
b Have a good/nice day.
c Have a good/nice time.
Have a good/nice holiday.
d Have a good/nice time.
Have a good/nice evening.
Have a good/nice meal.
e Have a good/nice weekend.

58 be (1)

1
b Happy Birthday!
You're 16 today!
c Hello. I'm John.
I'm a student.
d We're Japanese.
We're from Osaka.
e Mr Williams … Yes,
you're in Room 235.

2
b are
c are
d is
e are
f is

3
b She's a doctor.
c It's four o'clock.
d He's 24.
e It's a nice day.
f They're married.

4

b 3 It's
c 2 He's
d 4 She's
e 6 They're
f 1 It's

59 be (2)

1

b I'm
c I'm not
d I'm not
e I'm
f I'm not

2

b isn't
c isn't
d aren't
e aren't

Family 1: Alan, Flora, John, Julia
Family 2: Mary, Charles, Susie, Nick

3

b You're not ten. / You aren't ten.
c He's not German. / He isn't German.
d We're not Mr and Mrs Jones. / We aren't Mr and Mrs Jones.
e It's not 5 o'clock. / It isn't 5 o'clock.
f They're not new. / They aren't new.
g It's not a photocopier. / It isn't a photocopier.
h She's not his wife. / She isn't his wife.

60 be (3)

1

b Are you from Brazil?
c Are you Spanish?
d Are you married?
e Are you a teacher?

2

b Is the water warm?
c Are the beaches clean?
d Are the people friendly?
e Is the food good?
f Is it cheap? / Is the food cheap?

3

b Yes, it is.
c Yes, they are.
d No, he isn't.
e No, it isn't.
f Yes, she is.
g No, we aren't.

4

b Where are the Black Mountains?
c Who are the Sax People?
d Who is John Dando?
e Where is Gbinsk?
f What is a hammer?

61 There is/are

1

b There are four hotels.
c There are four shops.
d There's a/one car park.
e There are two campsites.
f There's a/one swimming pool.

2

b P
c P
d T
e P
f T

3

d There aren't any cats.
e There are two children.
f There's one hotel. / There's a hotel.
g There are four tables.
h There aren't any bikes.

62 Is/Are there …?

1

b Are there
c Are there
d Is there
e Are there
f Is there
2 d
3 f
4 b
5 c
6 e

2

b Is there
c Is there
d Are there
e Are there
f Is there

3

b How many showers are there?
c How many bars are there?
d How many rooms are there?
e How many baths are there?
f How many beds are there?

63 Present simple (1)

1

work; teach; go; like; speak

2

b P
c C
d P
e P
f C
g P
h C

3

b He drinks
c He watches
d He reads
e He studies
f He lives

4

b live
c work
d teaches
e teaches
f speak
g speak
h have
i studies
j goes
k speaks

64 Present simple (2)

1
b I don't eat
c I don't drink
d I don't have
e I don't speak
f I don't play

2
b I drink coffee. / I don't drink coffee.
c I work. / I don't work.
d I have long hair. / I don't have long hair.
e I speak Japanese. / I don't speak Japanese.
f I have children. / I don't have children.

3
b I don't know.
c I don't understand.
d I don't understand.
e I don't know.
f I don't understand.

4
b don't speak
c don't watch
d don't live
e don't know
f don't have

65 Present simple (3)

1
doesn't listen
doesn't watch
doesn't sit
doesn't read

2
b doesn't go
c doesn't have
d doesn't wear
e doesn't speak
f doesn't live
g doesn't play

3
b She likes cats.
c He doesn't like school.
d He likes pop music.
e She doesn't like children.
f He doesn't like birthdays.

4
b doesn't
c don't
d don't
e doesn't
They can all eat Pizza Al pollo.

66 Present simple (4)

1
b Do you read
c Do you drink
d Do you wake up
e Do you have
f Do you listen

3
lives; works; starts; finishes; earns; studies

4
b do you live?
c do you finish work?
d do you earn?
e do you study?
f do you study?

67 Present simple (5)

1
b Do they; No, they don't.
c Does he; Yes, he does.
d Does she; No, she doesn't.

2
b What does Eric Clapton play? 5
c Where do elephants come from? 1
d Where do Fiat cars come from? 2
e What does Ronaldo play? 6
f Where does the US President live? 3

3
b What time / When does the party start?
c What time / When does the train leave?
d What time / When does the train arrive?
e What time / When does the party finish?
f What time / When does the library open?

68 Present continuous (1)

1
b I'm eating
c I'm writing
d I'm drinking
e We're sitting
f We're listening
g We're eating
h We're playing

2
b I'm learning
c We're living
d We're working
e I'm staying
f I'm learning
g I'm working

3
b I'm not learning Spanish.
c I'm not studying maths.
d I'm not working in a restaurant.
e We aren't staying at a campsite.
f We aren't talking about Sue's sister.

69 Present continuous (2)

1
a She's reading; She's wearing
b He's standing; He's playing
c He's sitting; He's smoking

2

b They're drinking
c They're reading
d They're smoking
e They're eating
f They're laughing

3

A John
B Nick
C Alex
D Bill
E Peter

a isn't wearing
b is reading
c isn't talking
d aren't wearing
e are wearing
f isn't eating

70 Present continuous (3)

1

b Are we going home?
c Is the bus coming?
d Are you sitting here?
e Is he staying in this hotel?
f Am I going the right way?

2

… No he isn't
Yes, she is …
… No, it isn't
Yes, we are …
… No, they aren't

3

b it is
c I am
d they are
e it isn't
f she is

4

b What is she studying?
c What are they watching?
d Where is he working?
e Who are you writing to?
f Where are we going?

5

b What is he doing?
c What are they doing?
d What is she doing?
e What are they doing?
f What are you doing?

71 Present continuous (4)

1

b They're going to Miami.
   They're staying in an apartment.
c They're going to Singapore.
   They're staying in a hotel.
d They're going to Italy.
   They're staying in a villa.

2

b she's going to the sports centre
c she's having dinner
d she's going to Cambridge
e she's playing tennis
f she's having lunch
g she's going to a party

3

a When are you coming back?
b How are you getting there?
   Who are you going with?
c When are you going?
   Where are you staying?

72 Imperatives

1

a 2, 7   turn, wait
b 4, 5, 8 push, ring, close
c 3, 6   type, click

2

b Ring
c push
d Stop
e Type
f Turn
g Close
h Click

3

b listen to
c Come in
d sit down
e Come here
f Look at

4

✓ Go for walks.
✗ Don't work at the weekend.
✗ Don't eat late in the evening.
✓ Smile a lot.
✗ Don't watch TV every evening.
✓ Do sport every week.

73 *will* and *won't*

1

b won't
c will
d will
e won't
f won't

2

b They'll be there.
c She won't be there.
   She'll be in Hong Kong.
d They won't be there.
   They'll be on holiday.
e She'll be there.
f He won't be there.
   He'll be on holiday.

3

a will
b Will we/you; will
c Will it; No
d Will; they won't
e Will; Yes, she
f Will you; No

74 *I'll, I won't, Shall I …?*

1

b I'll
c I won't
d I won't
e I'll
f I won't

2

b Shall I give her (some) flowers?
c Shall I wear a dress?
d Shall I go with John?
e Shall I give her (some) chocolates?
f Shall I go by taxi?
g Shall I wear (some/my) earrings?

3

b Where shall we go?
c What shall I have?
d Where shall we sit?
e What shall I wear?
f Where shall I put the bag?

75 *can* (1)

1

b I can/can't ride a bike.
c I can/can't ride a horse.
d I can/can't drive a car.
e I can/can't swim.
f I can/can't speak Arabic.
g I can/can't play the guitar.

2

b She can drink.
c She can't drive a car.
d She can talk.
e She can't play chess.
f She can't ride a horse.

3

b Can you use a computer?
c Can you play the piano?
d Can you ride a bike?
e Can you ride a horse?
f Can you drive a car?
g Can you play chess?

76 *can* (2)

1

a … you can sit in Central Park and you can see the Statue of Liberty.

b … you can ride in a gondola and you can sit in Piazza San Marco.
c … you can sit by the River Nile and you can visit the Pyramids.

2

b You can put bottles here.
c You can't use your phone here.
d You can't take photos here.
e You can't swim here.
f You can smoke here.
g You can ride a bike here.

3

b Can I use
c Can I send
d Can I have
e Can I have
f Can I use

77 Asking for things

1

b Could/Can you bring me some water, please?
c Can/Could you give me my book, please?
d Could/Can you phone the doctor, please?
e Can/Could you open the window, please?
f Could/Can you bring me a sandwich, please?

2

Restaurant: an ashtray, the menu, the bill
Plane: a pillow, a blanket, a magazine
b Can/Could I have an ashtray, please?
c Could/Can I have the menu, please?
d Can/Could I have the bill, please?
e Could/Can I have a pillow, please?

f Can/Could I have a blanket, please?
g Could/Can I have a magazine, please?

3

Laura I'll have tomato soup, and then I'd like fish with potatoes, please.
Hamid I'd like tomato soup, and then I'll have green beans with potatoes and tomatoes, please.
Fatima I'll have salad with fish, and then I'd like chicken and salad, please.

78 Offers and suggestions

1

b Shall I buy some sandwiches?
c Shall I call the waiter?
d Shall I ask for the bill?
e Shall I open the window?
f Shall I make some coffee?

2

b Would you like to
c Would you like
d Would you like to
e Would you like to
f Would you like
g Would you like to

3

b Let's go for a walk. / Shall we go for a walk?
c Shall we go to a restaurant? / Let's go to a restaurant.
d Shall we go swimming? / Let's go swimming.
e Let's go shopping. / Shall we go shopping?
f Let's go to the cinema. / Shall we go to the cinema?

79 Question words (1)

1
b What's that?
c Where's that?
d Who's that?
e Who's that?
f What's that?

2
b What's your phone number?
c What's the weather like?
d What month is it?
e What's John like?
f What time is it?

3
b When is the party?
c Where is the meeting?
d What time / When is the meeting?
e When is the flower show?
f What time / When is the party?

4
b What sports do you like?
c What football teams do you like?
d What colours do you like?
e What writers do you like?
f What fruit do you like?

80 Question words (2)

1
a How can/do I; How much
b How far is it; How can/do I
c How can/do I get to; How far is it
d How can/do I get to; How much is it

2
b How are you?
c How old are your parents?
d How are your children?
e How old is your sister?
f How old is your house?

3
b Why is she having a party?   6
c Why is she learning Japanese?   2
d Why is he running?   3
e Why is he always tired?   1
f Why is the room cold?   5

Phonemic symbols

Vowel sounds

Symbol	Example
/iː/	sleep
/i/	happy
/ɪ/	dinner
/ʊ/	foot
/uː/	shoe
/e/	red
/ə/	arrive father
/ɜː/	work
/ɔː/	walk
/æ/	cat
/ʌ/	sun
/ɒ/	clock
/ɑː/	car
/eɪ/	name
/aɪ/	my
/ɔɪ/	boy
/eə/	where
/ɪə/	hear
/əʊ/	home
/aʊ/	cow
/ʊə/	euro

Consonant sounds

Symbol	Example
/p/	put
/b/	book
/t/	take
/d/	dog
/k/	car
/g/	go
/tʃ/	church
/dʒ/	age
/f/	for
/v/	video
/θ/	three
/ð/	this
/s/	sport
/z/	zoo
/ʃ/	shop
/ʒ/	usually
/h/	hear
/m/	make
/n/	name
/ŋ/	bring
/l/	look
/r/	road
/j/	young
/w/	wear

Index

The numbers in the Index are unit numbers, not page numbers.

Friday /'fraɪdeɪ/ **5A**
fridge /frɪdʒ/ **41B**
friend /frend/ 53B, **57D**
friendly /'frendli/ **46C**
from /frɒm/
  come from **66C**
  He's from ... **39A**
front /frʌnt/
  in front of **21A**
fruit /fruːt/ **42A, 42B**
fruit juice /fruːt dʒuːs/ **42A**
Furniture /'fɜːnɪtʃə/ 41
Future
  We're going ... **71**
  will, won't **73**

game /geɪm/
  computer game **30C**
garage /'gærɑːʒ/ **35C**
garden /'gɑːdən/ **35C**
garlic /'gɑːlɪk/ **42B**
gate /geɪt/ 23B, **36A**
geography /dʒi'ɒgrəfi/ **63A**
German /'dʒɜːmən/ **39A, 39B**
Germany /'dʒɜːməni/ **39A**
get /get/
  get (= buy, bring) **51D**
  get dressed **27C**
  get home **55A**
  get married **6B**
  get undressed **27C**
  get up **55A**
get there /get ðeə/
  How are you getting there? **71C**
get to /get tə/ **31C**
  How can I get to ...? **80A**
  How do I get to ...? **24A**
girl /gɜːl/ **25A**
give /gɪv/
  give (me) 51C
glass /glɑːs/ 14A, **44C**
  a glass of ... **14B**
glasses /'glɑːsɪz/ 25C, **27B**
go /gəʊ/ **50**
  go along, down ... **24A**
  go by (bus) **31B**
  go for (a walk) **50C**
  go into **50A**
go home /gəʊ həʊm/ **22C**
go + ...-ing 30B, **50C**
go to /gəʊ tə/ **50B, 50C**
  go to bed **55A**
  go to sleep **55A**

go to work **22C, 55A**
golf /gɒlf/ **30A**
good /gʊd/ **45A, 46A**
Good (morning) **48A**
good idea /gʊd aɪ'dɪə/
  That's a good idea 13C, **78C**
Goodbye /gʊd'baɪ/ **48A**
grape /greɪp/ **42B**
grass /grɑːs/ **36B**
great /greɪt/ **46A**
green /griːn/ **47A**
grey /greɪ/ **47A**
ground floor /graʊnd flɔː/ **2B**
guitar /gɪ'tɑː/ **30C**
gym /dʒɪm/ **13A**

hair /heə/ 25B, **26A**
half /hɑːf/
  half a kilo/litre of ... **42C**
  half past **3B**
hand /hænd/ **26C**
  shake hands **69B**
has /hæz/ **56, 57**
hat /hæt/ **27A**
have /hæv/ **56, 57**, 63A
  Can I have ...? **77B**
  Could I have ...? **77B**
  have (a party) **57B**
  have (an ice cream) **57A**
  have (dinner) **44A, 55A, 57A**
  Have a (nice time) **57D**
  I'll have ... **77C**
he /hiː/ **17B**
  he'll **73B**
  he's **58C**
head /hed/ **26A**
healthy /'helθi/
  a healthy diet **16B**
hear /hɪə/ **52A**
Hello /hel'əʊ/ **48A**
her /hɜː/ **18B, 19B**
Hi /haɪ/ **48A**
hill /hɪl/ **36A, 37A**
him /hɪm/ **18B**
his /hɪz/ **19B**
holiday /'hɒlədeɪ/ **71A**
  on holiday **6B**
  summer holiday **71A**
home /həʊm/
  at home **22C**
  get home **55A**
  go home **22C**
horse /hɔːs/ **36B**

ride a bike, horse **75C**
right /raɪt/ **24A, 24B**
  That's all right **48B**
ring (n.) /rɪŋ/ **40A**
ring (v.) /rɪŋ/ **72A**
river /ˈrɪvə/ **36A, 37A**
road /rəʊd/ **20C, 36A**
room /rʊm/ **41A**
  changing room **13A**
  double room **62B**
  family room **62B**
  living room **41A**
  single room **62B**
rose /rəʊz/ **34A**
round /raʊnd/ **26B**
run /rʌn/ 30B, **49C**
  go running **30B**
Russia /ˈrʌʃə/ **39A**
Russian /ˈrʌʃən/ **39A, 39B**

's (e.g. John's car) **19C**
salad /ˈsæləd/ **43A**
salon /ˈsælɒn/
  beauty salon **13A**
salt /sɒlt/ **44C**
sandwich /ˈsænwɪdʒ/ **43A**
Saturday /ˈsætədeɪ/ **5A**
saucer /ˈsɔːsə/ **44C**
sauna /ˈsɔːnə/ **13A**
sausage /ˈsɒsɪdʒ/ **65C**
say /seɪ/ **53A**
school /skuːl/ **29A**
  at school **22C**
  go to school **22C**
  language school **68B**
screen /skriːn/
  computer screen **72A**
sea /siː/ **37A**
season /ˈsiːzən/ **6C**
Seasons /ˈsiːzənz/ *6C*
second /ˈsekənd/ **2A**
secretary /ˈsekrətəri/ **29A**
see /siː/ **52A**
sell /sel/ **34A**
send /send/ **32B**
September /sepˈtembə/ **6A**
seven /ˈsevən/ **1A**
seventeen /ˌsevənˈtiːn/ **1A**
seventeenth /ˌsevənˈtiːnθ/ **2A**
seventh /ˈsevənθ/ **2A**
seventy /ˈsevənti/ **1B**
shake hands /ʃeɪk hændz/ **69B**
Shall /ʃæl/
  Shall I (go by car)? **74B**

Shall I (take your coat)? **78A**
  (Where) shall I/we (go)? **74C**
  Shall we (have a pizza)? **78C, 74C**
she /ʃiː/ **17B**
  she'll **73B**
  she's **58C**
sheep /ʃiːp/ **36B**
shelf /ʃelf/ **10B, 41B**
shirt /ʃɜːt/ **27A**, 33C
shoe /ʃuː/ **27B**, 33C
shoe shop /ʃuː ʃɒp/ **34A**
shop /ʃɒp/ **29A, 34**
  clothes shop **34A**
  flower shop **34A**
  go shopping **50C**
  shoe shop **34A**
shop assistant /ʃɒp əˈsɪstənt/ **29A**
Shopping /ˈʃɒpɪŋ/ *34*
shopping list /ˈʃɒpɪŋ lɪst/ **34B**
short /ʃɔːt/ **25B**
Short answers
  No, he doesn't etc. **67A**
  No, I'm not etc. **60A, 60C, 70B**
  No, I can't etc. **75C**
  No, I don't etc. **66B**
  No, I won't etc. **73C**
  Yes, he does etc. **67A**
  Yes, I am etc. **60A, 60C, 70B**
  Yes, I can etc. **75C**
  Yes, I do etc. **66B**
  Yes, I will etc. **73C**
shower /ˈʃaʊə/ **41B**
  have a shower **57B**
sign /saɪn/ 23B, 29A, **35A**
Signs /saɪnz/ **72A**
single room /ˈsɪŋgl rʊm/ **62B**
Singular and plural 10
sister /ˈsɪstə/ **28A**
sit /sɪt/ **49A**, 68A
sit down /sɪt daʊn/ **49B**, 72B
six /sɪks/ **1A**
sixteen /ˌsɪkˈstiːn/ **1A**
sixteenth /ˌsɪkˈstiːnθ/ **1A**
sixth /sɪksθ/ **2A**
sixty /ˈsɪksti/ **1B**
ski /skiː/ **30B**
  go skiing **30B, 50C**
skirt /skɜːt/ **27A**
sleep /sliːp/
  go to sleep **55A**
slice /slaɪs/
  a slice of (pizza) **43A**
small /smɔːl/ 26B, **45A**
smoke /sməʊk/ **69A**

snack /snæk/ **43C**

snow /snəʊ/ **38C**

sofa /ˈsəʊfə/ **41B**

some /sʌm/ **15**

   some + *plural* **12A**, 15A, 11D

   some + *uncountable* **14B**, **15B**

sometimes /ˈsʌmtaɪmz/ **9B**

son /sʌn/ **28A**

Sorry /ˈsɒri/ 13C, **48B**

soup /suːp/ **43A**

south /saʊθ/ **37C**

spaghetti /spəˈgeti/ **43A**

Spain /speɪn/ **39A**

Spanish /ˈspænɪʃ/ **39A**, **39B**

speak /spiːk/

   speak (French) **63A**, **75C**

spoon /spuːn/ **44C**

Sport /spɔːt/ 30

sports centre /spɔːts ˈsentə/ **35A**

spring /sprɪŋ/ **6C**

stairs /steəz/ **35C**

stand /stænd/ **49A**, 69A

stand up /stænd ʌp/ **49B**

star /stɑː/

   film star **17B**

start /stɑːt/ **4B**

   start work **55A**

station /ˈsteɪʃən/

   bus station **35A**

   railway station **35A**

stay /steɪ/ **68B**, **71A**

steak /steɪk/ **43A**

steps /steps/ 20A, 23B, **35C**

stop /stɒp/ **72A**

straight on /streɪt ɒn/ **24A**

strawberry /ˈstrɔːbəri/ **42B**

stream /striːm/ **36A**

student /ˈstjuːdənt/ 13C, **64A**

study (n.) /ˈstʌdi/ **41A**

study (v.) /ˈstʌdi/ **63A**

suburb /ˈsʌbɜːb/ **20C**

sugar /ˈʃʊgə/ **43C**

Suggestions 78

suit /suːt/ **27A**

suitcase /ˈsuːtkeɪs/ **27B**

summer /ˈsʌmə/ **6C**

summer holiday /ˈsʌmə ˈhɒlədeɪ/ **71A**

sun /sʌn/ **38C**

sun cream /sʌn kriːm/ **54D**

Sunday /ˈsʌndeɪ/ **5A**

sunglasses /ˈsʌnˌglɑːsɪz/ **33C**, **54D**

sunny /ˈsʌni/ **38C**

supermarket /ˈsuːpəˌmɑːkɪt/ **34A**, **35A**

sweets /swiːts/ **43C**

swim (n.) /swɪm/

   have a swim **57B**

swim (v.) /swɪm/ **49C**

   go swimming 30B, **50C**

swimming pool /ˈswɪmɪŋ puːl/ **35A**, 56B

Switzerland /ˈswɪtsələnd/ **37A**

table /ˈteɪbl/ **41B**

table tennis /ˈteɪbl ˈtenɪs/ **30A**

tail /teɪl/ **26C**

take /teɪk/ **51A**, **51B**

   take off (clothes) **27C**

   take (it) off (the table) **51B**

talk /tɔːk/ **53B**, 69B

   talk about **53B**

   talk to **53B**

tall /tɔːl/ **25B**

taxi /ˈtæksi/ **31A**

   go by taxi **31B**

   in a taxi **31A**

taxi company /ˈtæksi ˈkʌmpəni/ **29B**

taxi driver /ˈtæksi ˈdraɪvə/ **29B**

tea /tiː/ **42A**

teach /tiːtʃ/ **63A**

teacher /ˈtiːtʃə/ **29A**

teenager /ˈtiːnˌeɪdʒə/ **25A**

teeth /tiːθ/ **55B**

television /ˈtelɪvɪʒən/ **40B**, **41B**

tell /tel/ **53A**

   Can you tell me ...? **24A**

ten /ten/ **1A**

tennis /ˈtenɪs/ **30A**

   table tennis **30A**

   tennis court **13A**

tenth /tenθ/ **2A**

terrible /ˈterəbl/ 38A, **46A**

text (message) (n.) /tekst/ **32A**

text (v.) /tekst/ **32B**

Thank you /θæŋk juː/ **48B**

that /ðæt/ **13**

   (Who's) that? **79A**

   That's (right) **13C**

   That's all right **48B**

the /ðə/ **12**

theatre /ˈθɪətə/ **35A**

   go to the theatre **50C**

their /ðeə/ **19B**

them /ðem/ **18B**, **18C**

There is/are /ðeə ɪz/ /ɑː/ 61

   Is/Are there ...? **62A**

   How many ... are there? **62B**

   there's/there are **61A**

   there isn't/aren't **61B**

these /ðiːz/ **13**

they /ðeɪ/ **17B**
  they'll **73B**
  they're **58C**
thin /θɪn/ **26B**
Things /θɪŋz/ *40*
Things on the table 44C
think /θɪŋk/ **53D**
third /θɜːd/ **2A**
thirsty /ˈθɜːsti/ **48D**
thirteen /θɜːˈtiːn/ **1A**
thirteenth /θɜːˈtiːnθ/ **2A**
thirty /ˈθɜːti/ **1B**
thirtieth /ˈθɜːtiəθ/ **2C**
this /ðɪs/ **13**
  this (morning) **7C**
  this (summer, week ...) **7B**
those /ðəʊz/ **13**
thousand /ˈθaʊzənd/ **1C**
three /θriː/ **1A**
through (the gates) /θruː/ **23B**
Thursday /ˈθɜːzdeɪ/ **5A**
tie /taɪ/ **27B**
Time 3, 4
time /taɪm/
  a nice time **46B**
  What's the time? **3D**
  What time is it? **3D**
Time phrases 7
tired /taɪəd/ **48D**
tissues /ˈtɪʃuːz/ **40A**
to /tuː/
  (I'm going) to (the airport) **22B**
  (five) to (one) **3C, 4A**
today /təˈdeɪ/ **7B**
toilet /ˈtɔɪlət/ **41B**
tomato /təˈmɑːtəʊ/ **42B**
tomorrow /təˈmɒrəʊ/ **7C**
  tomorrow (evening) **7C**
tonight /təˈnaɪt/ **7C**
toothbrush /ˈtuːθbrʌʃ/ **34A**
top /tɒp/ **27A**
towel /taʊəl/ **54D**
Towns /taʊnz/ *35*
traffic /ˈtræfɪk/ **52A**
traffic lights /ˈtræfɪk laɪts/ **47A**
train /treɪn/ **31A**
  go by train **31B**
  on a train **31A**
trainers /ˈtreɪnəz/ **33C**
tram /træm/ **31A**
  go by tram **31B**
  on a tram **31A**
Transport /trænˈspɔːt/ *31*
tree /triː/ **36B**

trolley /ˈtrɒli/ **78A**
trousers /ˈtraʊzəz/ **27A**
T-shirt /ˈtiːʃɜːt/ **27A**
Tuesday /ˈtjuːzdeɪ/ **5A**
tuna /ˈtjuːnə/ **65C**
tunnel /ˈtʌnəl/ **23B**
turn (left, right) /tɜːn/ **24**
TV/television /ˌtiːˈviː/ /ˈtelɪvɪʒən/ **41B**
twelfth /twelfθ/ **2A**
twelve /twelv/ **1A**
twentieth /ˈtwentiəθ/ **2A**
twenty /ˈtwenti/ **1A, 1B**
two /tuː/ **1A**
type /taɪp/ **72A**

ugly /ˈʌgli/ **46C**
UK, the /ˌjuːˈkeɪ/ **75C**
umbrella /ʌmˈbrelə/ **27B**
uncomfortable /ʌnˈkʌmftəbl/ **46C**
Uncountable nouns 14
under /ˈʌndə/
  under (the bed) **20A**
  under (the bridge) **23B**
understand /ˌʌndəˈstænd/
  I don't understand **64B**
undressed /ʌnˈdrest/
  get undressed **27C**
unfriendly /ʌnˈfrendli/ **46C**
university /ˌjuːnɪˈvɜːsəti/ **63A, 63C**
up /ʌp/ **23B**
  get up **55A**
  wake up **55A**
us /ʌs/ **18A**
USA, the /ˌjuːesˈeɪ/ **39A**
use /juːs/ **76C**
usually /ˈjuːʒəli/ **9C**

vegetable(s) /ˈvedʒtəbl/ **42A, 42B**
Verb + -s 63B, 63C
very /ˈveri/ **45B**
video /ˈvɪdiəʊ/ **52B**
Vietnam /ˌvjetˈnæm/ **37A**
villa /ˈvɪlə/ **71A**
visit /ˈvɪzɪt/ **76A**
volleyball /ˈvɒlibɔːl/ **30A**

wait /weɪt/ **72A**
waiter /ˈweɪtə/ **29A**
waitress /ˈweɪtrəs/ **29A**
wake up /weɪk ʌp/ **55A**
walk /wɔːk/ **49C**
  go for a walk **50C**
wall /wɔːl/ **36A**
  on the wall **41C**

want /wɒnt/ **54A**
  want to **54A**
warm /wɔːm/ **38B**
wash /wɒʃ/ **55B**
  wash the dishes **78A**
wasp /wɒsp/ **47A**
watch (n.) /wɒtʃ/ **40A**
watch (v.) /wɒtʃ/ 30A, **52B**, 55B
water /ˈwɔːtə/ 14A, **42A**
way /weɪ/
  the way to (the station) **24A**
we /wiː/ **17A**
  we'll **73B**
  we're **58A**
  We're ...-ing **68A, 68B**
wear /weə/ **27A, 27B**
Weather 38
weather /ˈweðə/ **38A**
Wednesday /ˈwenzdeɪ/ **5A**
week /wiːk/ **7A**
weekend /ˌwiːkˈend/ **5A, 5B**
west /west/ **37C**
What ...? /wɒt/ **79A**
  What about ...? **73B**
  What colour ...? **47C**
  What do you do? **29C**
  What (music) do you like? **79D**
  What is/are ...? **60D**
  What (day) is it? **79B**
  What shall I/we ...? **74C**
  What time does ...? **67C**
  What time is (the meeting)? **79C**
  What's (the weather) like? **79B**
  What's your address? **79A**
When ...? /wen/
  When are you ...? **71C**
  When does ...? **67C**
  When is (the meeting)? **79C**
Where ...? /weə/ **79A**
  Where are you staying? **71C**
  Where do you work? **29C**
  Where is/are ...? **60D**
  Where is (the concert)? **79C**
white /waɪt/ **47A**
Who ...? /huː/ **79A**
  Who are you going with? **71C**
  Who is/are ...? **60D**
Why ...? /waɪ/
  Why is he running? **80C**
  Why is the shop closed? **80C**
wife /waɪf/ **28A**

will /wɪl/ **73**
  He'll be there **73B**
  It will rain **73A**
  will not (= won't) **73A, 73B**
  Will you phone? **73C**
wind /wɪnd/ **52A**
window /ˈwɪndəʊ/ **41C**
wing /wɪŋ/ **26C**
winter /ˈwɪntə/ **6C**
with /wɪð/ **25C**
woman /ˈwʊmən/ **25A, 10C**
women /ˈwɪmɪn/ **10C**
won't /wəʊnt/
  I won't (go swimming) **74A**
  It won't rain **73A**
  She won't be there **73B**
wonderful /ˈwʌndəfəl/ **46A**
wood /wʊd/ **36A**
Work 29
work (n.) /wɜːk/
  at work **22C**
  before/after work **4D**
  finish work **55A**
  go to work **22C**
  start work **55A**
work (v.) /wɜːk/ **29, 63A, 64A**
  Where do you work? **29C**
  work for **29B**
  work in **29A**
would like ('d like) /wʊd laɪk/ **54C**
  Would you like (a drink)? **78B**
  Would you like to ...? **78B**
write /raɪt/ **55B, 68A**
write to /raɪt tə/ **32B**
writer /ˈraɪtə/ **17B**

year /jɪə/ **7A**
  (10) years old **8A**
yellow /ˈjeləʊ/ **47A**
Yes /jes/
  Yes, he does etc. **67A**
  Yes, I am etc. **60A, 60C, 70B**
  Yes, I can etc. **75C**
  Yes, I do etc. **66B**
  Yes, I will etc. **73C**
  Yes, please **78B**
you /juː/ **17A, 18A**
  you're **58A**
young /jʌŋ/ **45A**
your /jɔː/ **19A**

Acknowledgements

We would like to thank Alison Sharpe, Anna Teevan and Jamie Smith for their invaluable help in developing Language Links into its final form. We'd also like to thank Tony Garside for editing the final version, TEFL Tapes and Kamae Design. We are also grateful to Cambridge University Press for permission to use the Cambridge International Corpus.

We would like to thank the following for their very generous help with photos and drawings for the book:

Albert Blausmoser; Noirin Burke; Gabriella Doff; Natasha Doff; Theodor Ferner; Stefan, Gaby and Tommy Gulár; Michael and Madeleine Sergi; Dieter Schenk; Jamie Smith; Sabine Staebe; Ingrid Tancsics; Jenny and Til Waldhier; Dragutin Zaharias.

The authors and publishers are grateful to the following illustrators and photographic sources:

Action Plus pp. 14 (Glyn Kirk), 88 (Darren Carroll/Icon/Tiger Woods); Alamy Images p. 47 (National Motoring Museum/Motoring Picture Library/Volvo); Altrendo Images/Getty Images p. 48; Associated Press p. 168 (George Harrison); Botanica/Getty Images p. 84 (Brian Leatart/Caribbean); Bridgeman Art Library pp. 108 (Bathers at Asnieres, 1884 (oil on canvas), Seurat, George Pierre (1859-91) National Gallery, London, UK), 126 (Arrangement in Grey and Black No.1, Portrait of the Artist's Mother, 1871(oil on canvas), Whistler, James Abbot McNeill (1834-1903)/Musee d'Orsay, Paris, France, Giraudon), 148 (Woman Reading a Letter, c.1662-63 (oil on canvas), Vermeer, Jan (1632-75)/Rijksmuseum, Amsterdam, Holland, The Card Players, 1893-6 (oil on canvas), Cezanne, Paul (1839-1906)/Samuel Courtauld Institute of Art Gallery) (www.bridgeman.co.uk); Corbis pp. 20 (George Hall), 26 (Randy Faris/Sarah, Bill Varle/John, RayMcMahon/Alice), 27 (Laura Doss/baby at 5 weeks), 43 (Michael Boys/apple pancakes), 49 (Larry Williams), 52 (Norbert Schaefer/modern family), 55 (Jeremy Bembaron/Corbis Sygma/DJ), (Rob Lewine/daughter), 61 (Anna Palma/glasses, Neal Preston/bearded man), 62 (Neal Preston/Arnold Schwarzenegger), 66 (Bettmann), 71 (Laura Dwight), 88 (David Bowie), 120 (Kristi J. Black), 136 (Gabe Palmer/ violinist), 160 (Don Mason), 168 (Frank Hurley/Endurance), 168 (Bettmann/Amundsen); Food Features p. 43 (orange cheesecake); Foodpix/Getty Images p. 143 (Benjamin F Fink); Getty Editorial pp. 47 (Robert Atanasovski/Maria Joao), 62 (AFP/Mick Jagger), 127 (Yussef Allan/Jordanian Palace), 129 (Clive Brunskill/Maria Sharapova); The Image Bank/Getty Images pp. 27 (Dan Bigelow/young baby and 5 year old), 47 (Ryan McVay/writer), 60 (Ryan McVay/Anna), 136 (Yellow Dog Productions/Baseball man); Marcos Silviano do Marco p. 162 (www.ipanema.com); Mark Ruffle p. 26 (boy and girl); Photodisk Green/Getty Image p. 133 (Adalberto Rias Lanz/ Sexto Sol); Powerstock pp. 29 (Age fotostock), 60 (Mauritius/John), 117 (Super Stock/Bill); Rex Features pp. 88 (CLY/Juliette Binoche), 127 (SIPA/King Abdullah II and family); Robert Harding World Imagery/Getty Images p. 84 (Robert Francis/Vietnam); Royal Geographical Society p. 162 (Shackleton); Sheldon Memorial Art Gallery p. 34 (Edward Hopper/Room in New York); Stock.xchng p. 72 (Blazej Pieczynski/bike, Stefan Suciu/bus); Stone p. 27 (Gabrielle Reeve/baby at 5 months), 47 (David Roth/dad), 60 (Rezza Estakhrian/Juan), 61 (Christa Renee/long hair), 70 (Richard Ross), 84 (Orion Press/Switzerland), 152 (David Hanson); Stone + p. 60 (Karen Moskowitz/Yoko), 61 (Shannon Fagan/Amy); Taxi/Getty Images pp. 61 (Emily Shur/Jon), 101 (David Norton); Time & Life Pictures/Getty Images p. 117 (Gjon Mili/milk); Travel Ink pp. 20 (Biniam Ghezai/Big Ben, Ronald Badkin/Eiffel Tower and Gondola, Britt Willoughby Dyer/Colisseum, Robin McKelvie/Parthenon), 146 (Biniam Ghezai/Big Ben, Ronald Badkin/Eiffel Tower), 168 (Luc Janssens/Atonium).

Illustrated by Gillian Martin; Kamae Design; Nick Schon; John Storey.